Audry Maphosa
& Grace Maworera

Tales of Living in Diaspora

16 candid short stories of life in diaspora

Copyright © Audry Msipa and Grace Maworera

Published by: Diaspora Quest Publishing

First publication: 2018

Audry Msipa and Grace Maworera have asserted their right to be identified as the authors of this work in accordance with the Copyright, Designs and Patents Act 1988.

A CIP catalogue record for this title is available from the British Library

ISBN 978-1-9164378-0-7

Book Design by Loulita Gill Design

Printed and bound by IngramSpark, www.ingramspark.com

www.talesindiaspora.com

Acknowledgements

From the conception of an idea to the completed book you now hold in your hands, this project has taken almost a year. It took the combined efforts of many people, and we would like to take this opportunity to recognise them and extend our thanks.

First and foremost, we would like to thank the sixteen anonymous contributors who gave of their time and effort to share their stories. It took courage to be honest and vulnerable, and we appreciate their willingness to get involved with this venture. We are truly grateful that they believed in the vision we had for this book – without them, it would not have happened. In addition, we would like to express our gratitude for their future donations (from the proceeds of this book) to a charity that supports healthcare improvement in developing countries.

To Alison Carson, our editor: thank you for editing and re-editing all of the stories, compiling the book and making suggestions on the overall structure. We really appreciate your flexibility, patience and encouragement. Thank you very much. We look forward to working with you on future projects.

To Loulita Gill at Loulita Gill Design: thank you for your unwavering support and advice throughout this process.

From designing the cover and transforming edited work into text for hard copies and eBooks to creating our website and helping with marketing advice, your help has been invaluable. Thank you very much.

To the Diaspora Quest Publishing Team: thank you for publishing this book.

To all those unsung heroes around the world whom we have not mentioned ... you know who you are: thank you for all of your support.

More
Tales in Diaspora

This book is the first in a series of six about life in diaspora. Our future publications have the following working titles:

Tales of Nursing in Diaspora
Tales of Success/Succeeding in Diaspora
Tales of Marriages/Relationships in Diaspora
Tales of Raising Children/Parenting in Diaspora
Tales of Working in Diaspora

Are you are currently living in diaspora? Would you like to share your experiences in one of these upcoming books? If so, please email us at **tales@talesindiaspora.com** and indicate the publication for which your story is suitable.

All contributors will be remunerated and credited, but please note that most stories will be published anonymously. However, if you are contributing to the book about succeeding in diaspora and you would like people to be able to contact you for more information, then please include all relevant contact details in your tale.

Contents

Introduction

It's no secret that immigration has increased exponentially in recent years. *The International Migration Report 2017* by the United Nations states that there are approximately 258 million international immigrants, which is an increase of 49% since 2000. Ten per cent of these immigrants are refugees or asylum seekers.[1] No doubt, figures will continue to increase in the years to come.

People who change their location from one continent in the world to another are not only affected themselves, either positively or negatively, but the local communities they leave and enter are also affected. Thus, immigration has become significant to every human in the worldwide community to which we belong.

When one leaves their motherland to reside in another land, it is usually in the hope of attaining a better life, though several other factors may also be at play, including the economy and politics. Some choose to migrate, while others are forced. For

---

1 https://www.un.org/development/desa/publications/international-migration-report-2017.html [accessed May 2018]

instance, some people choose to venture to distant shores to improve their levels of education or career opportunities, whereas others are forced to leave due to political instability, poverty or war.[2] Regardless of the reasons, the journey is rarely easy. Invariably, immigrants encounter various hurdles and challenges along the way.

This book aims to communicate some of the reasons and challenges experienced by individuals living in a foreign land – living in diaspora. It is a compilation of sixteen stories, each revealing the realities of immigration, the highs and lows of leaving home and country for another land.

The stories contained in these pages will inspire and challenge readers, and some accounts may even bring laughter. Above all, these are testimonies that show what it takes to overcome the challenges of immigration. As well as being a book to enjoy, it also serves as unique research, offering first-hand evidence of the immigration process and the challenges therein.

All of the contributors are anonymous. To protect their identities, identifiable features have been removed and pseudonyms are used in place of real names. All content reflects the views and opinions of the individual contributors.

***

The journey of a thousand miles begins with a single step.

LAO TZU

---

2 http://www.bbc.co.uk/schools/gcsebitesize/geography/migration/migration_trends_rev2.shtml [accessed May 2018]

1

The Journey Continues

I cannot say I am a traveller or that I had anything in mind while growing up about travelling the world. But sometimes, life gives us a piece of something we desire, even when the desire is subconscious. Yes, I was destined to travel, and I'll let you into a little secret: life does not keep me in a country for very long!

There are many reasons why people migrate or travel; my reason for migration was simply destiny, it was never a choice. However, after all these years, I have realised that people who migrate are no ordinary people! There is something in them – some level of courage and passion, and it compels them to move out of their home and their comfort zone. By saying this, I am not referring to myself, because my moves have been destiny and not a choice made by me … each time!

By birth and origin, I am an Indian. My travels began at just three months old. My father was working in the United Arab Emirates, and my mother and I flew there to accompany him. The days of mass migration in my part of the world had stopped, and life had been peaceful. People now migrated for better opportunities, a better life, or to support their families back home. Soon, my father decided he wanted to move to Saudi Arabia, so we all moved again. I was very young, so I do not remember my days in the UAE.

Life was good in Saudi Arabia. I did the majority of my primary education there. Life was also simple: during the week, I went to school, and at weekends, we went shopping or played in the park. Life was different back then, and it was not as glamorous as it is now. The hotel culture, mall entertainment, cinemas and mobile phones did not exist. For families, there were only two options of entertainment: visit a park or visit friends. It might be hard for someone who has not lived in that era to imagine what it was like. Certainly, it was very different from how I lived the second half of my lifespan.

A few years later, we moved back to India so that I could attend high school. This was not an uncommon practice among those living in the Middle East. In those days, once children reached high school age, they moved back to their home countries while their fathers stayed behind to work and earn. It is still true in Saudi Arabia today, as many expat families return home for further education.

By this time, I had two younger brothers, so my mother travelled with three children. My parents loved India, and so did my brothers and I. For us siblings, we always knew that one day we would head back to our country of origin, but we had never actually lived there, just visited, so we had a perception of India as being a fun place. We had loved playing with cousins during vacations and spending time with our grandparents and other relatives. I know that I do not speak just for my family; it is for any family living outside of India, even now! Little did we know that life is serious there and that kids actually study! I completed my schooling years and attained a master's degree in a western region of India where my family still lives. Then came the big changing point: I married and migrated to England. My husband was already living there, and I never knew that things would change so much for me as a person.

Everything was different in England, from the weather to the lifestyle and culture. I was amazed to find that there was a governing system that people trusted and followed, unlike India, where there is not a system for anything. I often applaud Indians for being a breed of human beings who are extremely patient and can adapt to any adverse condition without even thinking or complaining.

There was something about the UK that made me love it from the start, though getting used to the weather took time. There is a lot this country gave me. No matter what people say about living in western countries, I felt safe. I was relaxed and at ease. People are trustworthy, and they rarely cheat. After several years in the Indian subcontinent, I had become very sceptical about people and what they wanted from me.

We moved around from city to city for my husband's job. Over the years, I got used to the simple life in England. Everything about the place had become mine – how things worked, the lifestyle, the weather … everything. Yes, the weather as well! The cold and wet weather didn't bother me anymore. The one thing I really struggled with was accents! It took a while to get used to one, and before I got the hang of it, we moved again and faced another challenging accent!

I met some amazing people on my journey; they never made me feel like I was away from home. They were my family now, and that sense of belonging was complete. My children were born in England and got into the education system. I completely got used to the environment, which was no longer new. My roots were back in India, but my branches were breathing in a new space. We did visit India every year, and the joys of travelling with young children made us swear not to travel the following year, and yet we did, year after year. The thing that I love about the UK is that it accepts everyone, no matter where they are from, and it gives each person the freedom to continue being themselves.

Years passed, and we made the important decision to become British citizens. It was a big step, but we have never regretted it. I felt like I belonged in England more than anywhere else. My simple migration changed from immigration to citizenship. When I think back, the two most valuable things this place gave me are the taste of independence and a vision to see life from a different perspective. Once I had these, it was impossible to go back to my old self. These two virtues carved me, polished me, made me shine, and they defined me as a person.

The reality of diaspora showed itself in ways I did not imagine. The years of absence from my original country created a gap, and there was a clear difference in my thought processes to the rest of my people at home in India. I was suddenly short of common topics to discuss with my own family. There was also a difference of opinion, and it is bound to happen to anyone who has moved out of his or her place of origin. The reason is simple: new experiences give a person a new platform to see and think. My children understand where they come from and can speak and understand their mother tongue, but English is their first language. I believe they will take goodness from each country and culture and become better individuals.

Just when I was feeling settled in my British status and could see a future in the country, things started to change for us. This time, life was taking me full circle. New ambitions and aspirations had started to tickle my husband's mind, and that is a dangerous sign for me. He wanted a change and took a job in the UAE. I was heading towards the place where I started. I didn't want to move; yet somehow, got convinced. It was harder than any other move I had made.

I felt that my independence would be taken away and that once again, I would be dependent for little things. I had become used to going out on my own, shopping and driving etc., and I believed that all these flavours of independence would be taken away. The reason I thought this was due to my experiences of living in the Middle East. I had been completely dependent upon my father, and I had observed that females only ever went out if they were with a male member of the family. If it wasn't the father, it was the husband. That was how it was until recently. To be honest, it didn't make a difference back then. As a child, I saw things through my parents' eyes, and I didn't mind or question it. But now, I had a new set of eyes and an addiction to independence. All of my childhood memories made it difficult to make the move. Some women are happy with the dependent life, but I am not one of them.

However, when we moved, my thoughts and fears were pushed away, and I was proved wrong. We settled in Dubai, and remarkably, I found it not too different from England regarding independence. I was so pleased to discover that my independence was not compromised. I could drive, do things on my own, and even walk alone on the street at 10:30pm without fear (which was not possible in England). And much like England, the UAE absorbs people, no matter where they come from. It didn't take long for me to start loving it! It just goes to show why the UAE has been such a popular diaspora destination for many people for many years. When I went to view a school for my children, I noticed that it had more British students than a school in Britain!

For all of its similarities, I quickly found that the lifestyle is very different. It's an amazing city that never sleeps. It has taught me new terms, like the 'Dubai Stone', which is a reference to people gaining a stone in weight while in Dubai, partly due to eating out being de rigueur. I also learned about a class of expat ladies called 'Jumeirah Jane' as mentioned in the novel by Kyra Dupont-Troubetzkoy. It is not fiction! You will find them having fancy brunches every day and wearing branded clothes from designers like Louis Vuitton, Gucci, Fendi and Prada. And let's not forget their manicured nails and meticulous makeup that would send models running for a few tips! The word 'luxury' starts in Dubai. The city gives a whole different meaning to glamour and luxury, be it in architecture or people. Everything is larger than life, with huge buildings, big aspirations and undefeatable ambitions. It all makes one look timid, yet it keeps individuals longing to rise, to achieve and to reach high. Such is the feel of this place. The sky is now very different from how I had left it years back; now, the buildings reach the sky!

Culture shock didn't hit me in any of the countries I lived in … until I took my children to school in Dubai and found maids and drivers – not parents – dropping off and collecting children. Yes, life here for locals and expats is dependent on maids, aka magic wands!

In three years, this place has moulded my personality and filled me with aspirations. It has made me dream big, yet I miss the little things from the UK – buying good quality clothes (even from supermarkets), easily returning items to shops, and the ease with which money was credited back to my account. It's just the simplicity of a few things that make me turn back and look at the past.

My children love it here and don't miss England much, though they do want to visit. For them, the UK is their home. We go to India every year so they can visit their grandparents. They know the place they have come from, the place where they belong, and the place where they now live. It has slightly confused them … I know this because I have heard them describing themselves to other people! However, this move has enriched them with experiences of a lifetime. When their school celebrates 'International Day' they have the choice to dress up as an Indian, British or local Emirati citizen. Diaspora has given them this diversity. In essence, they are natives of three cultures.

I know my identity is not lost. The religion, the traditions, the food we eat at home is still the same, but what has changed is the vision and the thought processes. The richness of experiences resonates in our minds and shows its glimpse in our personalities. We have accepted the new culture within us, which is a mirror of the places we have lived and the goodness we have absorbed from each place.

This is the true beauty of diaspora. In one lifetime, it scatters you like little stars everywhere and still makes you shine! Yet, once again, I dread the tickle in my husband's mind, and every time he says, "The world is my home," ... the journey continues!

2

God Bless Our Country

―――――――――

"So, I'm going to the UK!" It just felt unreal, as I had tried twice before to acquire a visa to the UK but had no luck. Part of me wanted to stay in my mother country since I had my mum and son there as well as a job that I enjoyed dearly. What more could I have wished for really? Another sensible part of me was telling me that I should grab this opportunity, as the UK was a land of milk and honey. "How will my dear friend feel if I suddenly say I'm not coming?" I asked myself. My friend had worked so hard to get me a visa, so how could I let her down?

One day in November some years ago, I boarded Air Zimbabwe destined for the United Kingdom. Yes, I decided to go to the milky land. Landing at Gatwick at 5:00am, I suddenly had an excitement within me, and my expectations were very high. I remember a lovely lady who I met on the plane ... she was so good to me. She actually waited for me to pass through immigration. May the good Lord bless her and her family (unfortunately, I lost her number before I reached my destination).

I remember travelling on a coach and thinking, "Wow, the seats are so comfortable, and there are only ten people on the whole bus!" This didn't happen where I had come from; there, the bus only leaves the station when it is full ... of both humans and livestock.

After a week of absorbing my new environment, I was honestly thinking about going back home. It was cold, raining, dark and very miserable. To make matters worse, I didn't think people in this country ate whole meals or proper food. This was because my friend never seemed to have any food in her house. Of course, I couldn't explore far as I did not wish to get lost. It was only after I talked to my cousins about my living conditions, in particular, my nzara (hunger), that I moved to another city and realised that food was plentiful in the UK, and there was a vast variety one could buy.

Mind you, since arriving, I did not have any of my travelling documents as my dear friend had said she would keep my papers for safety (how naive I was then). That meant I could not look for a job in the new city I had moved to. Fortunately, I managed to get a temporary job through a lady from my church. When I got my first pay cheque, I quickly repaid my friend most of the money I owed her for covering my expenses to the UK. I hoped she would give me back my passport, which she did. She never mentioned that she had taken my passport to guarantee that I would pay her back, but I suspected that was her reason. I knew I would pay her back at some point for the air ticket since that had been our agreement. She knew perfectly well I had come with very limited funds, as I had exhausted most of my savings to make sure my mum and son were comfortable back home.

The experience I had with this friend made me focus on what I wanted to achieve. I only had a couple of months left on my visa, so I knew I had to act swiftly to get a stable job. I bought a newspaper, turned the pages straight to the job section, and I remember one that really caught my eye. There was a name to contact, so I dialled the number and asked to speak to 'Agy'. The lady on the other end was very polite, but what she said to me made me feel so stupid. Apparently, 'Agy' stood for 'agency'. Anyway, we live and learn.

I did not give up. I then searched for all nursing and residential homes in the area where I lived and rang them, asking for a job. One of them called me in for an interview. The interviewers asked me for my documentation, and I gave them receipts from the post office with proof that I had sent my documents to the Home Office. They rang me two days later to offer me a job. I worked at that residential home for six years. I really enjoyed working there, and I was made to feel like I was part of the team. But they didn't know that I had no valid papers since the Home Office had rejected my application for asylum. However, I appealed that decision and was successful years after I had resigned from that job. The very idea of ever being granted asylum seemed like a dream when I was going through the appeal.

I managed to enrol my son in a good school in Zimbabwe and look after my mum and siblings. Throughout this time, I had loads of challenges, but I still carried on. Being in diaspora was an eye-opener for me as an individual. It was really hard at first, especially because I couldn't understand what the British people were saying … they spoke so fast! So, whenever someone spoke to me, and I didn't understand, I would say, "Pardon?" in order for them to repeat themselves and to give myself ample time to mould my accent. I guess on my part, I was trying too hard to fit in, which I eventually did. But you can take the girl out of Gweru, but you can never take Gweru out of the girl.

I have had disappointments from relationships, friends and even relatives, but I guess it's the world we live in that is just so selfish. As I grow older, I tend not to tolerate anyone who has no values. In this part of the world, it is challenging to trust fully, as most individuals are self-centred. Money has broken friendships and relationships. During the early years of being in the UK, I had bad experiences with serial debtors. I used to send cash to relatives whenever I could, on the agreement that they would pay me back when they could. I believed that they needed the money for meaningful stuff for their households, but little did I know that my money was being used for their own pampering! I've had lots of my hard-earned money squandered this way, as they did not keep their side of the bargain. I have since written off these debts as I feel it is best to do so.

Now comes the weather. I have never gotten used to the cold and gloomy days in this country. I always dread them. Everyone looks so miserable and very uptight. However, when it's spring and summer, all the darling buds of May come out, bright and shining, and people even begin smiling … yes, smiling. I really enjoy the summer months as I get to visit the seaside. My visits to the beach and weekend getaways are special because I have an amazing travelling companion ... yes, you've got it, I met a man, and we travel together. We have travelled to many different places, and we continue to do so whenever we get a chance. Sometimes, it becomes challenging to travel as I work shifts, yet he has a 9-5 job. However, we balance it quite well.

Transport in the UK is amazing. It's very reliable and affordable when travelling locally, but you still come across people who complain. If one doesn't own a car, like me, buses run throughout the day and into the night in some areas. The only problem nowadays, however, is the crime rate. There are lots of casualties because of stabbings and shootings. Though not where I live.

Living in the UK can be very lonesome, especially if all your family is back home. There are times when I feel so homesick that, if I'm on my own, I actually cry for hours. I don't, however, cry in front of anyone, unless I'm with my dear sweetheart. At times, it is difficult to explain to him why I'm crying or feeling low, and it can be hard for him to understand. There are times when my son needs some stuff that I can't provide and that makes me feel sad. My son is the main reason why I came here, and he is the reason I keep going.

Recently, I lost my younger brother. He had a heart condition that was diagnosed very late. His death was a big blow for me and my family back home. I never suspected that he wouldn't recover. I remember ringing home every couple of hours to check on his progress. Whenever they told me he had eaten four spoonfuls of porridge, I would be so hopeful that there was an improvement. Following his death, I fell into a deep depression, yet at the same time, I was very functional … I still am. When I think of that period, I feel very angry and frustrated, and I wonder whether things would have been different if I had returned home. Maybe with the knowledge I have acquired here, I could have challenged the care that he received back home. I could have also challenged how there is not enough support for relatives of patients receiving palliative care in Zimbabwean hospitals. Being here and working in various areas of healthcare has exposed me to so many skills, from ensuring patient safety to communicating effectively with relatives. I have a lot of respect for the NHS. In this country, the NHS will provide all the support needed for both the patient and the relatives. They also provide support for families who have lost a loved one. In this country, one doesn't have to hesitate to seek medical attention since it's free, and it can be accessed easily … one can actually go to see a doctor for a cold. These are all services that don't exist in Zimbabwe.

Then comes corruption. There is corruption in this country, but at a lower percentage compared to my home country. Back home, one has to pay someone to get their own money from the bank, whereas here, there are loads of banks to choose from. Here, we also have cash machines outside most bank buildings, which hardly ever run out of cash. There are also vast supermarkets with all sorts of foods – a person can choose from the good quality, medium or value range – so really why should I complain? There has not been one single day that I have gone hungry unless I've chosen to do so.

Culture. The culture here is very different from where I come from. A mother once told me that her sixteen-year-old daughter's boyfriend was staying in her house for the night, and not just in her house, but sharing a bed with her daughter. In my country, this is unheard of. Here, teenagers get home after midnight, and some parents will not even ask where their children have been. This used to trouble me, as it was a real culture shock. I've also noticed that a lot of people swear and shout. At first, I used to think that some people here are hard of hearing, as they always seem to speak very loudly and swear a lot. I don't like swearing, and I will never get used to it. This is because when I was young, my parents always used to tell us that swearing was unholy. Yet, most people are very friendly. This includes work colleagues, neighbours and even strangers. However, one does meet one or two who have the stiff upper lip (will never smile).

In conclusion, the United Kingdom is a very beautiful and welcoming country. I really enjoy it in the UK, and I have enjoyed all the years I have spent here. However, I do miss my home country, especially my family. I do hope that one day, when the political situation is better and the economy has stabilised, I will return to the land that was once called the breadbasket of Africa: Zimbabwe. God bless our country (Ishe komborereyi nyika yedu)!

3

I Am My Brother's Keeper

I long to hear my name said in my native language. Often, people ask if they can call me by a shorter, easier version of my name instead. Am I supposed to say no and cause them a sprained tongue and a kink in the neck? At least it's not as bad as my cousin's surname, which is mispronounced beyond all recognition! "Sure," I say. Although, in my heart, I hope that one day someone will surprise me by saying my name in Shona.

I am from Zimbabwe and was born in the capital city, Harare. My parents met in the UK back when Rhodesia was under British rule. They had both been given the opportunity to study and work abroad, where they decided to get married, buy a home and start a family. I am the last of three children. I have two older brothers, and am the only girl … and still spoilt!

When Rhodesia gained its independence and was renamed Zimbabwe in the early 1980s, my parents returned home to the breadbasket of Africa. With our country thriving, my siblings and I went to private boarding schools where we only saw our parents three times each term. These fixture weekends were packed full of fun. We visited relatives and caught up on the coolest games, music and dances. The summer holidays were great because we would travel to Gweru or Bulawayo to spend several weeks with our cousins. It was a joy playing in the 5-acre gardens, having feasts in the *muhabhurosi* – mulberry tree, and helping our uncle on the plot *tichisakura* – ploughing of sorts. Birthday parties, kitchen parties, baby showers and weddings were tremendous fun with hundreds of relatives often in attendance. It is this family time, the unity, that I would miss and long for once I migrated to the UK and Canada.

During the years of land seizures by the government, there was a mass exodus of both black and white people from Zimbabwe due to the politics, shortage of fuel and skyrocketing cost of living. My mum took the opportunity to immigrate to the UK, once again, for work. My eldest brother went with her and enrolled at a university. My father remained in Zimbabwe, and later my parents' marriage dissolved. My other brother and I also remained in Zimbabwe – at boarding school. My summer holidays now meant travelling to the UK to be with my mum instead of trips to Gweru and Bulawayo. While it was difficult to no longer spend fixed weekends at home with my mum, the prospect of spending six to eight weeks in the United Kingdom where the Queen of England lives and bragging to my friends about it made the separation easier to deal with. It was, however, difficult for my mum to be away from two of her children, from her extended family and from home. She worked in a care home and lived in a single bedroom on the premises. All of her belongings were in two suitcases.

It was not too long after my last A-Level exam that my mum told me to pack up all of my belongings and join her in the UK. For immigration purposes, I needed to be there before my eighteenth birthday. The stamp in my passport from the immigration officer at border control reminds me how I was unhappy to be in England this time. Actually, I was furious! The sixth form balls in Zimbabwe come after the students' exams. Not only did I miss my own ball, but I also missed the opportunity of attending other balls from the boys' high schools. The worst part of it all was that I arrived in England on a one-way ticket. I had no time to say goodbye to my friends and extended family. To them, I disappeared and went off the grid. The thought of not going back and not being with my friends was a tough pill to swallow. I had grown up in a boarding school, and during the period my mum was far away, my friends had become my other family.

Boarding school benefitted me greatly; it taught me survival skills and how to conform to the system, the surroundings and the culture of the environment. However, being in the advanced country of England made integrating very intimidating. I was no longer surrounded by mates my own age, but by the whole world! Navigating through the social spectrum was my biggest challenge. For the first time in my life, I felt like I didn't fit. I wanted and needed to be with my own people.

The culture of disrespect where elders are called by their first name, the disassociated families, the liberties, the loose morals and the reckless definition of fun left me telling my mum that I would like my tertiary education to be in Canada rather than in the UK. Since my other brother had been in Canada for two years and was enjoying being oceans away from home, I believed I would, too. At that time, I did not realise that there was little difference between the two first world countries. First world countries have their first world problems. In my naive mind, I thought it would make another great story to tell my friends and that I would be envied by them. The reality was that I had no one to tell since I couldn't afford long distance calls every day, and the letter writing and telegrams gradually reduced in frequency. By the third and fourth month following my cord from Zimbabwe being cut, I finally begun to heal as acceptance letters from universities were replacing the telegrams from friends and family.

The drive from the airport to where I would stay in Canada filled me with such joy and peace. With its vast and spacious land, Canada felt like home. The pace was slower than the buzzing English cities, and folks were friendly and quite apologetic. Conversations became much more interesting since I had the British accent, and everyone loved it. I thrived once again as I bloomed in the institute of higher learning. It was what I had been accustomed to at boarding school. I realised then that my whole life had been in preparation to live away from my parents, yet I still yearned for their company, advice and encouragement. Just as I did in high school, I only went 'home' (which was the UK since that is where my mum lived) twice a year: once during the summer holidays and then again at Christmas. During my university years, I learned that my family means everything to me. I praise the communications industry for long distance telephone cards, Skype, Facetime, WhatsApp and Facebook, all of which enable us to keep in touch with our loved ones.

My greatest difficulty in Canada was coming to terms with the difference in culture concerning family values, especially the importance and expectations of family and friends. Non-immigrant families seem to be estranged from one another quite easily, even within the core family. Brothers who live in the same city can go for decades without visiting or even speaking to each other. Parents and grandparents are put in nursing homes too quickly, left to the care of nurses instead of family members. You would think, seeing as though the subdivisions in suburban areas are open, much like the villages in Zimbabwe, there would be a close community. In Zimbabwe, we have electric gates and durawalls (brick fencing) separating our homes, yet our doors are open to each other, and one can expect a steady stream of visitors at a moment's notice. There is no need to schedule a day to visit; impromptu pop-ins are the norm. However, in Canada, I found that the focus is on the nuclear family, and these individuals enclose themselves within the four walls of their home. One must call in advance for a visit as if booking for a doctor's appointment.

I also found the culture of independence difficult – although being the baby of the family could have contributed to my apparent 'neediness'. Independence – the ability to rely on oneself – is embedded into the western culture. Their mottos could well be: 'Do all you can for yourself before bothering anyone else with the problem' and 'Make sure you always look out for *number one* – yourself!' I grew up in a culture where families were structured in such a way that parents, siblings and relatives are identified and named according to the role they play in your life. *Amai* is a mother and *Baba* is a father. For aunties, we say *Amai-nini, Amai-guru* or *Tete* – meaning those who will be there for you as a mother to care for you. For uncles, we say *Babamukuru* or *Babamunini* – those who will be there for you as a father. We also have other titles for aunties and uncles who have the role of grandmothers and grandfathers – *Ambuya* and *Sekuru*, respectively. Cousins, and even neighbours, can also be given the title of mother, father, brother or sister. I never knew my parents', aunts' or uncles' first names until my late teenage years, and even to this day, some of my aunts I only know as *Amai-nini Amai "Nhingi"* (Aunty, the mother of my cousin).

Of course, when I was growing up, I called my siblings and cousins who were my age or younger by their first names. Titles are only conferred upon an individual when they reach adulthood, and especially when one is married and has children. Husbands and wives no longer address each other by their first names but as *Amai* and *Baba*! Titles are names of honour and privilege; they declare the role and responsibility that a person has to their own household as well as to the extended family.

In Zimbabwe, we all play an important part in each other's families. No one is spared of this responsibility. No man is an island. As a people, we all have a responsibility to have a positive impact on each other and to help each other along the way. It takes a village to raise a child, truly. Daycare for babies and toddlers happens within the home; either a family member or a live-in hired help will take care of the growing children. The community comes together to raise a child to be a loving, well-mannered and well-behaved individual. But in Canada, children can call social services just because they are upset with their parents, and the parents are then investigated to determine whether they are fit to continue parenting that child. And when one is having a difficult time in life, psychologists and psychiatrists are called to talk through the issue and devise a treatment plan. These professionals thrive because the citizens of this country are independent and shut off from their own families who could help. My family is structured in such a way that we not only have familial roles, but these roles are similar to the government and law structure: there is a head of the family (the father; the firstborn male succeeds him), a parliament that decides the state of affairs (grandparents and their siblings), and elders who are judge (both parents) and jury (aunts and uncles). If you ever need help, all you need to do is look within your family. We are all one big family, with God at the centre of our lives uniting us all in love and care for one another.

I hold my native name and my role very dear to my heart. Whenever I have the opportunity to talk about my culture to non-immigrant friends or colleagues, I gladly take it. Often, their initial response is, "What a burden that must be." But when they hear me boast about how close my family is and how we rely upon each other, I am met with admiration … and many have expressed the desire to have such a family themselves.

There are great opportunities in western countries as seen in education and the various careers that follow, especially for those considered to be 'unlearned'. The school systems are designed to leave no child behind, even those with learning difficulties. There are special schools and classes for those with autism and

ADHD, those who would have otherwise been classed as a *benzi* – 'fool or madman' with very few prospects for their future. I was surprised to find that *anaSisi vemba* – maid services, garden boys aka landscape technicians, construction workers, carpenters, plumbers and the like can be more successful than what we consider the elite professions: doctors, lawyers, accountants etc. Those looked down upon have an opportunity to make the best of their lives, exceeding those with Dr, Esq or CA attached to their name.

My mother worked very hard for our success, and we achieved it. She spent years working double shifts back-to-back, week after week, month after month, year after year, sacrificing sleep to pay our international school fees. All of this was to ensure that we had all we needed as we navigated ourselves along the path of international students and onto the road of becoming citizens of a country that would give us a better life. Today, I am privileged and blessed to see her joy and peace every day when she hugs me after a long day at work. She is reaping the benefits of her labour in my very home. She traded her family for mine where she enjoys the company of her son-in-law and her granddaughters. We, in turn, traded our green passports for blue ones and now travel the world with her. I am who I am because my mother invested in the future I live every day. The future she saw when she packed her bags and said goodbye to her husband and country is what I live today. However, it was not only for her children's future but also for her entire extended family, because we live a culture of 'I am my brother's keeper', which is deep within us, reaching out to help Zimbabwe from abroad. I am who I am because she invested in her legacy of love, to be in unity with her family and to practise godliness ... because this is the way to live as a Zimbabwean in a foreign land.

4

My Memoirs of the Immigration Process

I was very fortunate to have a privileged childhood in Bulawayo, Zimbabwe. I have three younger siblings, two sisters and one brother. My parents got divorced when I was thirteen, and my father then moved to the UK a year later. I lived with my mom, stepdad and siblings in a big house with an acre of land and a swimming pool. We would spend weekends camping with my cousins and their friends who were 5 years older than me, which seemed such a big age gap back when I was thirteen. I had a real crush on one of my cousin's male friends, but never in a million years would there have been any romance due to the age difference. I would go off to climb rocks and explore all day long without a worry in the world, apart from coming across the odd scorpion or hearing the monkeys and baboons calling out loudly. We never had mobile phones; in fact, we never even dreamed of such things.

Life was good. However, whenever my stepdad had too much to drink, he turned violent. He never hurt us children, but hearing the fighting and cries from my mother and then seeing her bruised hurt more than his physical blows ever could have.

They were very dark moments in my childhood; memories that will always haunt me. I tried to block it out of my mind, but the more time passed, the more it ate away at me.

The previous year, when I was twelve, my grandparents were killed in a car crash involving a lorry going through a red traffic light. It affected me negatively, and my schooling suffered. I was due to start high school, but my mom wanted me and my sisters to attend a convent school that combined junior and high school education. I was supposed to start in Form 1 (first year of secondary school), but my entry test results were low, so I had to repeat Grade 7 (last year of primary school). By the time I had reached Form 3, I had made up my mind about two things: I wanted to become a hairdresser, and I wanted to get away from my stepdad. I was already sixteen because of the repeated year of schooling, and I was legally allowed to leave school despite not taking the final examinations. I told my mom that I wanted to visit my dad in the UK and possibly attend college there, so she bought me an air ticket and let me go. Now that I am a mom myself, I realise this was a very brave thing for her to do.

At the very tender age of sixteen, my life changed dramatically as I flew unaccompanied from Harare, Zimbabwe to London on a three-month holiday visa. I had very mixed emotions. I was excited about travelling and seeing my dad who I hadn't seen for two years, but I was also sad, as I had just said goodbye to my mom and younger siblings. My main memory of that flight was sitting next to a man who was very broad shouldered and tall so took up a lot of my space as well as his own. Our seats were at the back of the place in the middle section. I was in the second seat, and he was in the aisle seat. I chuckled to myself and thought, "Just as well I am short and don't need much space," as my feet didn't even reach the floor! Anyway, this man was rather inebriated, to say the least, and he was making a real nuisance of himself. So much so, that when he went to the toilet, another man sat opposite him asked me if he was with me, and I said, "No!" Then he asked if I wanted him to 'sort him out' ... oh, could you imagine an argument mid-air? So I said, "Don't worry, I am going to go to sleep now," which I did. While we were flying over the Sahara, we hit some turbulence, and the 'fasten seatbelt' lights came on. The drunken man next to me woke me up saying, "Put your seatbelt on, we are going to crash." "Great!" I thought, "I would rather not have been woken up if that is the case." Thankfully, not long after that, he fell asleep, so the rest of the flight was uneventful.

Heathrow was a very cold and frosty -3 degrees. Such a contrast from the 34-degree temperatures I was used to, so needless to say, I felt freezing cold! While we drove to my dad's home in the south of England, I was amazed at the sight of snow lying on the side of the roads.

I kept in touch with my family in Zimbabwe through telephone calls. It was a ten-minute walk to the nearest phone booth, and it was expensive. I remember seeing the credit disappearing rapidly on the digital screen, and I would hurry to say everything I wanted to say before being cut off. Then I would walk slowly back to my father's house with tears rolling down my cheeks feeling very homesick. We also wrote letters, which took two or three weeks in the post to be delivered and received. It was always a joy to receive a letter that was folded in three and sealed around the edges (because it was an airmail letter and envelope in one – you don't really see these anymore due to the marvel of emails). Occasionally, I received a letter from the young man who was my teenage crush back when I was thirteen. He was an apprentice in Zimbabwe, and consequently, was bound to the country for 8 years on a very low wage so he could not afford to come to the UK for a holiday. All apprenticeships in Zimbabwe were for 4 years, and the following 4 years were to serve the country in that trade. For the entire 8 years, the rules stated that a person could not leave the country for more than two weeks at a time, and only twice a year. Also, there was a ceiling on earnings. All of this helped me make the decision to stay in the UK and go to college. But first, I had to sort out my visa. As time went on, the letters from the young man became less and less, and then we lost contact.

As I was on a holiday visa, I needed to change my visa. I was entitled to British citizenship through my grandparents, but I had to get the ball rolling quickly, so I phoned the Home Office and explained my situation, and they made an appointment for me to go and see them. It was a much easier process than it is now, but a much longer one because all correspondence was by post and phone calls … there was no internet then!

So off I went to London. I had to find my way to Lunar House in Croydon, which has etched memories of anticipation in my mind.

On my first visit, I had to queue in a very large, hall-like room for hours. I was amazed at the variety of people there; I saw every type of person from a punk to a transvestite (it was my first ever sight of the latter). I found it all very intimidating, especially since I had come from a convent school and had been used to my mom doing all the official things for me. Eventually, I got to see a Home Office officer and aired my case. He said that I need certified copies of all the birth and marriage certificates of my grandparents to apply for an ancestry visa, all of which I could obtain through the registry office in Liverpool. This process took quite a long time, a good couple of months.

When I finally got the paperwork, I had to go back to the Home Office and pay for my indefinite leave to remain status, which I think was around £180. Then it was a waiting game. Several months later, I received a letter to say that I was eligible and that it was being processed. This meant that I was allowed to work. So I found myself a job as an apprentice in hairdressing, earning £40 a week. By this time, I was renting my own accommodation, so I had to pay for that, too. I did some babysitting in the evenings just to try to make ends meet.

One day at work, I was shampooing the hair of a client, and he started chatting about Zimbabwe. He asked me some very specific questions about my passport and visa, explaining that I couldn't work if I had the wrong type of visa. It turned out that he was a custom's officer, and when he said that I could potentially be breaking the law, my heart sank, and my stomach turned. I was so nervous about breaking the law and the consequences of doing so. I certainly didn't want to be deported, which he said could be the result. I told him that I had applied for an ancestry visa and had been given the go-ahead to work … boy, oh boy, was I scared, but because I had already received a letter about my indefinite leave to remain, everything I was doing was legal.

After about 18 months, my passport was stamped with my indefinite leave to remain. Then, after five years of living in the UK, or three years of being married to a British citizen, I had the right to naturalise and become a British citizen. At that point, I could not afford it due to being an apprentice.

At age twenty-two, I did get married to a British citizen, but it wasn't until we wanted to go on an overseas holiday years later that I naturalised and became a British Citizen. And it was on my own grounds of being in the country for more than 5 years. Back then, it was a very understated process; I hired a solicitor, went to court and swore allegiance to the country while holding a Bible in my right hand. Then I had to send off a form with a payment of around £180. A couple of weeks later, I received my naturalisation certificate in the post. Nowadays, a person is required to attend a citizenship ceremony, and they receive a coin as well as a certificate.

So, I am now a British Citizen. I do consider the UK as my home, and I do not regret the move. However, Zimbabwe will always be in my heart. There are days when I feel very homesick and yearn for weekends of camping. Saying that … I was fortunate to go back to Bulawayo a couple of years ago, and I didn't cope too well with camping or the creepy-crawlies – I have become a creature of comfort now! I do wish I could let my two daughters have a similar childhood to what I had in Bulawayo. They were carefree, happy days … but is that because we were children and never had economic or political worries?

I achieved my hairdressing qualifications, and I have been in the industry for 26 years now, and I still love every day of my job. I have since divorced. Four years later, through the marvels of social media, the young man I had the teenage crush on back in Zimbabwe got in touch with me. I am so happy to say that he is now my husband and is in the process of becoming a British citizen himself. The whole process is a lot more involved and a lot more expensive. We have had several trips to the Home Office. Lunar House in Croydon has changed, but the building still brings back all those memories of when I went there almost 30 years ago. The entrance is a bit like going through customs at an airport – everyone has to walk through metal detectors and have their bags scanned. There is now a number system to see a customs official, so it is a much smoother process and not so daunting. I think the craziest thing my husband has had to go through for his spouse visa is an English speaking test. This is despite that fact that English is his first language! I am glad to say that he passed with a distinction.

It is still a five-year process for my husband to obtain indefinite leave to remain status, but it is now split into two equal intervals, so after two and half years, he will need to reapply for his spouse visa, which will cost in the region of £1,800. He will also have to complete the 'Life in the UK' test afterwards to become a citizen … I'm so glad I never had to go through all of that!

I don't think I would have the nerve to immigrate again, but I do not regret making the move when I was sixteen. I consider myself lucky that I have the best of both worlds. I can go on holiday to Zimbabwe to be in my home country with my relatives; and in the UK, I can buy some of the things that I miss, such as sadza, cream soda and biltong. I love my life here in England, but I'm also happy to be able to get my Zimbabwe fix.

5

The Grass Always Looks Greener on the Other Side

I was born in Kenya to a very large family. My father has four wives, and I was one of 24 siblings. I grew up in a very beautiful rural area. Having attended boarding school from the age of five, I attained my first degree in mathematics and computer science before coming to the UK. I worked briefly in Kenya, for one of the biggest insurance companies in Africa at that time. But I lost my job when the company went bust due to corruption. The CEO, who helped bring the company down, was then promoted to be the CEO of another parastatal company, later becoming a government minister. This sets the stage as to why I moved from my beautiful nation.

My journey to the UK was nothing other than miraculous since it was very difficult to obtain a visa. I had no job, no money, and I was a single mother of a young boy. I had to send my son to a boarding school so that he had somewhere safe to stay for more than nine months of the year. I was also aware that I needed to be able to support my parents as they became older. Most of my siblings were school-aged so were not earning and both of my parents were unemployed because they were past employment age. My eldest sister was already in the UK and was working as a registered general nurse. She would visit us back home, and from our conversations, her lifestyle appeared to be good. Little did I know that it was not easy for her.

I had never ever thought I would want to settle in a country with a cold climate nor one full of unfamiliar people in terms of colour, culture, religion etc. I had travelled abroad to India, Bangkok and Dubai for small business ventures, but even from these experiences in warmer climates, I had no desire to live outside of Kenya. However, it was rather obvious that this was going to be my only way out of the cycle of poverty.

My journey to the UK started after my cousin and I were thrown out of the home we were sharing. The landlord had been reasonable with us, but since we were unable to afford the rent, he couldn't continue keeping us as tenants. Following this, I was homeless for a prolonged period and experienced all the shame that comes with it. I had become a Christian by then, and I took my faith very seriously. Through trusting God, I was able to get a new passport and the money to purchase my ticket to the UK. It sounds simple, but there is no other explanation for it. The visa office was where I experienced my first miracle. Other people were being refused visas, but the young, white lady doing the interviews took a liking to me, and I got my visa with no problems. The next step was to get the ticket. This happened miraculously too, as friends I had not been in touch with for some time phoned me out of the blue and informed me they were all sending me money for my ticket. It was all too much for me to even believe. I then travelled to the UK on a visitor's visa. It was May.

Upon arriving in London, I experienced a bit of a setback. I was supposed to be met by a friend, but she had not checked the flight details and didn't know which terminal to collect me from. I had no idea where she was, and I had no phone on me. By chance, I met a very kind Kenyan man at the airport, and he helped me until I was able to re-connect with my friend. We then travelled together on the bus to a city in the south west of England. I remember the shock I felt when I saw London for the first time; I felt disappointed because it was not as nice as I had expected it to be. I was comparing it to other places I had been to, such as Dubai and Cape Town. Other than that, the trip was uneventful. All the trees looked grey, the weather was grey, and I was extremely cold. This is laughable because I now find May to be such a beautiful and pleasant month. In fact, it is one of my favourite months as I love nature, and I love the changes that take place from March onwards culminating in May. The countryside looks idyllic, birds return from their winter's migration, flowers bloom, butterflies flutter and much more.

Settling down was not easy. Most of the good things my friends had promised did not exist. Initially, I stayed with three friends. They allowed me to stay with them for a few weeks, and then somehow, they kicked me out. This was when my third miracle took place. I met a stranger, who took me to an organisation supporting homeless people and refugees, and I was offered a room to sleep in. I don't know who this stranger was, but exactly three months after arriving in the country, I was granted indefinite leave to remain status. Yes, you can say that again! I have, therefore, never experienced what most immigrants go through, as I was not without status for long. I knew then that my young son could eventually join me in the UK. He was doing extremely well at his school and was almost always top of his class. I did miss him very much, and I missed my parents and my siblings, too.

My caseworker at the Home Office, who had been very supportive, said that all he wanted from me was to do well, go back to university and be a useful member of society. I never forgot his statement, and throughout all these years, I have truly tried to be a part of the British community.

My first experience of work was quite awful. I got a job on a mushroom farm. The place stunk like a skunk, and the people were mean. Two Somalian men picked me up early in the morning, then I was on my feet from 7:00am until 4:00pm, with only two very short breaks in-between. The place was freezing cold because temperatures were maintained at 5 degrees. I could not believe what was happening to me; having studied a maths degree in Kenya and having been one of the best students in the country during my school years, even managing to get a place in one of the most prestigious national schools, here I was, among many other foreign workers, weighing mushrooms destined for the supermarkets! I quit on the fourth day and was never paid.

My second job was in the care industry, and this was even worse. I was sent to work in a nursing home, and I was so scared when I saw the old people – they looked grey, and I could not help but think they were dead. Also, the nurses were horrible, and I felt they did not treat the old folk as people at all. It was my very first night shift, and I cried most of the night, at one point hiding in a huge cupboard!

The next day, I decided that I was going back to Kenya, and I phoned my dad. He was very encouraging, and he reminded me that Rome was not built in one day. I went through this kind of state every now and then during my first year in the UK, but I realised I needed to get used to my new life and try to settle down. I joined an employment agency and was offered work in a large mental health unit. It was there that I met my future husband, but that is another story entirely. I am now married to one awesome, amazing, white man, who is way beyond what most women would imagine. God has been with us on our journey, and we still seek for more of Him in our lives.

My first experience with public transport was quite something. I sat on the bus, and despite it being full, no one sat next to me. I soon learned that this was going to be the way it was, and I determined that I would buy my own car, which I did fairly quickly. I had other racist experiences from time to time, but nothing major. I once had an outburst with an older nurse, who I told in no uncertain terms that I was not her little slave girl. She understood and kept her distance. I also determined that a low standard of living would not be my portion, so I started making plans to move forward, trusting God to open doors of opportunity for me.

The opportunity presented itself the following year when I was invited to an interview by an organisation that was seeking to employ black and minority ethnic (BME) workers within a drug and alcohol clinic. There were 37 applicants, and 2 of us were chosen. I had never met anyone who used drugs, I had no friends who smoked cigarettes, and I never had consumed much alcohol. However, I truly enjoyed the job. The clients really liked me, and they made me believe I could do the job. It was ironic that I was more liked by the predominantly white drug addicts than I was by other 'normal' people. It was tough, though. I had an amazing supervisor who supported me to study mental health nursing at university. I found the course quite basic because my first degree had been quite challenging.

I must admit that when I moved to the UK, I had no idea what I was looking for; I only knew I was running away from the poverty at home. Yet, I missed Kenya so much, and still do. I have settled down in the UK, and I do have a good life, but I always dream of going back to Kenya. In recent years, I have visited Kenya twice every year, and I always feel depressed and sad when I return. If someone was struggling and wanted to try things in another country, I doubt I would advise them not to do it. However, I do believe that most immigrants need to go back to their homeland. We are accepted in our own countries, and that's where we can make a difference.

There is a lot to learn in the UK and in other parts of the world, but it would be better still if that knowledge were taken back to base. I love many things about the British, including the respect men have for women. I love their politeness, even if it is a bit of a pretence. I love the way people do research into everything, and most things they advise upon are based on research. I love the way they experiment with lots of different foods, and how seriously they take nutrition and exercise. I love the way they have systems that work, and I admire how their leaders can easily recognise when they need to leave office and will not hold onto power. I like the roads and the discipline of drivers, instead of chaos. I appreciate how history has been preserved throughout the country. I admire the vision behind the NHS, despite all of its troubles, and I wish something like this could be available for my own people. But even with all these good things, I would rather be in Africa with people of a familiar background. My country is still so amazing. The grass always looks greener on the other side. I would rather be in Kenya.

6

I Still Love My Motherland

When I first tried to enter the UK, I was denied entry, unfortunately. My stepbrother and I had travelled together from Zimbabwe on visitor visas. We had hoped to have the opportunity to assess what we could do in the UK to develop ourselves. The economic crisis in our homeland was in its early stages. We were both nineteen and had finished high school.

The immigration officers who dealt with us when we arrived felt that we were not truthful about our purpose of entry as visitors. They believed we were political espionages acting for ZANU-PF! They cited our well-spoken English and the amount of money we had as the main reason for their suspicions. We had about £400 each in bank drafts and about £100 each in cash. Our payslips also indicated we were earning about $30,000 per annum (Zimbabwean dollars), which at that time, was a lot of money for the ordinary folk back home. The immigration officials claimed that all of this was above the standard of the ordinary Zimbabwean citizen. In addition, we were unable to answer many of their questions regarding the places of interest we would be visiting. I can't remember exactly which places we stated we would visit, but I know we didn't have much knowledge about tourist attractions except for Buckingham Palace, the London Eye, the Millennium Dome and Trafalgar Square. Subsequently, we were deported. We returned to Zimbabwe on the same plane that had brought us to the UK.

The economic situation in Zimbabwe continued to deteriorate. Six months after our deportation, my whole family decided to migrate. My parents' minds were set on moving to the United Kingdom. Dad had just retired from his full-time job, so they sold the family business and closed everything down. Soon after, we migrated to England as a family unit. As was common during that time, we came as visitors with the intention of renewing our visas as students once my parents, two of my siblings and myself had enrolled at a university. My parents only planned to stay for about a year, to see us settled, then they intended to migrate elsewhere. I looked for a job straight away so that I could be self-sufficient and lessen the burden on my parents who were trying not to touch their savings. This was despite the fact that employment was prohibited. I managed to get a job working 2 to 6 hours per day. This gave me the opportunity to assist my parents with whatever I could on a weekly basis. After some time, the hours occasionally increased to 6 to 9 hours per day, allowing me to save some money for my university fees.

Living in the UK wasn't an easy transition for my family. We had been used to a more luxurious lifestyle in Zimbabwe. We had always had a cleaner, a nanny, a gardener as well as others to help with various things, as needed. I also found it very hard to adjust to the weather, the taste of food, travelling on public transport, the work I was doing, and the busyness of everyday life. I also found it difficult to adapt to the smaller living spaces. I had anticipated big, spacious bungalows and detached homes, only to find lots of terraced houses and flats! This was a big shock to me! Of course, I had seen pictures of UK housing in magazines and books, but the reality of it had never sunk in. And I found the roads very narrow compared to what I was used to, and I honestly thought that I would never be able to drive in this nation. All of this and more meant that I had to ask many questions as I went along. It was a steep learning curve.

I remember needing to photocopy a document. I went to a shop that advertised photocopying, and the shopkeeper directed me to the copier. I had no idea what to do! Back home, the staff in the shops would do the photocopying for the customer. I also had to learn the value of the British pound. One morning, I turned up at the bus stop at 6:00am with a £50 note! Needless to say, the bus driver did not have sufficient change, and I had to alight from the bus and buy something from a nearby newsagent to get change.

The whole move was taxing, emotionally, psychologically, mentally and physically. I missed my friends, my home life and just the comfort of being in my own country. I lost about 8kg in weight during those first six months.

Six months later, when my visa was due to expire, I had managed to secure a university place to study for a diploma in nursing, and I was awarded a bursary. By this time, I had found my own accommodation and was a lot more settled. My visa status then changed to a student visa, which meant I could legally work for 20 hours each week during term time and more during holidays. This meant that I was very busy, studying full-time as well as working part-time to supplement my bursary income.

Living alone and studying brought two unique challenges. Firstly, I couldn't cook, since my mum, sisters or home help used to do the cooking when I lived at home. Secondly, I was not well versed in using a computer, so I spent a lot of time in the library learning how to use one and practising my new skills.

My parents didn't need to support me anymore. Instead, I was now also helping to support some of our extended family in Zimbabwe. Things were so bad for some of them, to the extent that they could only afford porridge for breakfast and one main meal at the end of the day when everyone was back from work or school. I'm glad I was able to help in the little way that I could. On completing my studies, I got job and a five-year work visa.

Zimbabwe was a great country to live in during my early childhood years. Things were so good that I never imagined or dreamed of settling anywhere else. Unfortunately, the Economic Structural Adjustment Programme of the early 90s, a drought, and a series of other events thereafter was disastrous to the economy: the country that was once the breadbasket of Africa started importing food and grain from other countries, employment became scarce, crime rose rapidly, and brain drain increased as professionals sought greener pastures in other countries. The invasion of farms owned by white farmers in 2000 was a chaotic and destructive move. Land was given to poor black people who were not prepared and did not have the know-how of large-scale farming. At the same time, farmers with decades of agricultural experience left the country. Consequently, harvests shrank and the nation began to undergo food shortages. Supermarket shelves were empty, rampant inflation took over, and the economy declined further. Though rich in natural resources, the nation lost the benefits thereof. The ruling party subjected the nation to torture, murder, corruption and manipulation. Zimbabwe was suspended from the Commonwealth, and international sanctions were imposed on it. Life expectancy rates also plummeted to an average of about forty years. A promising country had been destroyed. It was a sad situation. It is a pity that things got that bad.

I don't regret migrating to England. Initially, I thought I would go back to re-settle in my motherland after 5 to 10 years. This thought no longer exists. I'm grateful for the many opportunities the UK has given me, opportunities I would never have had in Zimbabwe. I have worked as a nurse for around 15 years now, and during that time, I managed to pursue and complete a master's degree so as to enhance my practice.

Everything about my immigration to the UK has been a big eye-opener, and should I ever decide to return to Zimbabwe, I know I will be taking back a wealth of knowledge and experience that will benefit the community and society there. I still love my motherland and visit every now and again. However, I'm now married, have children of my own, and we're all very happy to settle in England permanently. My siblings also have families of their own now, and most of our aunts and uncles and their families have since settled in the UK as well. Over the years, we have established a network of friends and close relationships with fellow Zimbabweans and local people, making us part of a vibrant and diverse community. Nevertheless, I still shed tears for my beloved Zimbabwe.

7

A Journey of a Thousand Miles

"The journey of a thousand miles begins with one step." This statement constantly replayed in my head like the melody of a favourite song. Contrary to popular belief, I matured to realise that the hurdles faced while embarking on this journey are not 'obstacles' but 'opportunities for growth'.

Losing a father at a stage when I was shaping to be the man I aspired to be and having no validation from that role model affected my psychological and physical development. Although some may argue that a mother can serve as both parents, I disagree. I often wondered who would teach me how to chop firewood, skin a cow, or better yet, how to treat a woman. My life vision started to get bleaker with every breath I took. I tried to seek positivity from the economic environment, but all I saw on the news were headlines such as, "90% of the population unemployed!" and "Galloping inflation set to crumble economy." As if that was not enough, then came the long, winding queues for basic commodities that were abundant on the black market at astronomical rates. This was the onset of the economic downturn that would plague the once breadbasket of Africa: Zimbabwe.

My high school professor drilled the concept of 'opportunity cost' into my heart and mind during my Foundations to Economics course. It didn't take me too long to realise that I had no alternative but to take my talents elsewhere. Thankfully, my mother taught me to focus on fixing the present to have a brighter tomorrow. This, she said, was better than joining the many who were constantly worried about what had happened and what would happen in the future. Simple as it sounds, it appears to be the hardest piece of wisdom for many to adopt.

I migrated to the United States of America during the famous economic downturn in Zimbabwe when escalating inflation was rampant. During that era, any chance to migrate was considered a blessing. Hell, even the governor of Reserve Bank himself probably had no idea how much his lunch would cost the following day! Our plight was a new case study for the world to analyse; a situation like it had not been documented anywhere in the history of economics. After months of acquiring the sought-after foreign currency, I finally secured enough for what the Americans called the first semester of university. I had been offered a partial waiver scholarship, which meant that I only had to fund half of my tuition fees and accommodation expenses, and the other half was paid by the university. Heaven knew how the rest of my tuition would be funded, but I was determined to grab the bull by its horns as soon as I landed.

As a young man hungry for success and determined to make life better, not only for the future generations but also for the family unit that had moulded me, I was thrilled upon hearing about the scholarship. Packing 19 years' worth of belongings into a 23kg suitcase and a 7kg carry-on bag had my mind racing. Besides the practicalities of travelling, I was also unsure about leaving. I had assumed various roles since my father's passing – who would take my place? Yet the devastating thought of leaving my mother, my little brother and two sisters hit me even harder. "Should I go?" I kept questioning my decision. Again, my mother's words made the difference. She assured me that everything would fix itself and that it was my time.

Life in university is always great, especially for a smart, hard worker. I was fortunate enough to have positive friends around me. Not only did they invite me to their homes during the Thanksgiving and the festive season, but they also wanted the best for me. I also had a cousin in New York City who occasionally invited me to the Big Apple to keep my inspiration levels up. The more I travelled, the more I learned that finances were necessary to facilitate a positive holiday experience. Odd jobs seemed only good for the short-term since they could do no more than finance the remainder of my fees and living expenses when combined with family contributions. Earning more money was not possible since the Department of Homeland Security had capped student working hours to twenty hours per fortnight during each semester. Violation of this rule meant the risk of deportation. It was a hurdle for most international students as most of us were struggling to make ends meet. Nevertheless, the 'Braveheart's' breached the law and were ready for deportation … if it ever came! I could not risk it, there was too much to lose.

The 'land of the free' has abundant opportunities available for those who yearn for them … supposedly. This is what has enticed several immigrants to America, and it still is. However, graduating from university is the ultimate test of endurance for most international students. Not only does one face the reality of the system, but individuals must also make decisions that will affect one's 'success' in America either positively or negatively. Every step of the journey matters. At the time, inadequate career counselling led to several students relying on the advice of peers regarding how best to navigate the system once they had graduated. Despite the job market having suitable vacancies, candidates were required to have a valid work visa, which many of us did not have. The other alternative was for an employer to sponsor a foreign employee, which would give the worker a visa that allowed them to stay and work for a certain period of time. However, even this was not straightforward – the most lucrative vacancies usually required candidates to have significant work experience first. How does an international student who has just graduated have a valid work visa or extensive work experience? What a predicament!

Living a life where tomorrow is not guaranteed can be a nightmare. It felt like I was living in limbo. And I found myself in an almost perfect romantic relationship at this critical stage in my life. However, as they say, it takes two to tango. I did not commit enough to the relationship because I was constantly worried about my visa. "Should I just marry her and get my paperwork sorted?" I thought to myself. My moral code wouldn't let me. Even looking at my furniture was frustrating; I could afford to spruce it up, but I constantly thought about what would happen if I had to leave the country. As for my choice of vehicle … well, that's another story for another time.

Ethics and moral values were constantly tested while trying to find a way to stay in America permanently. Despite this, we still had to live and enjoy the dream while it lasted. Every day was an unwelcome reminder that our days were numbered. I will never forget my first experience at an NBA championship game in the Philips Arena. Whoever thought I'd see Dwyane Wade and LeBron James doing what they do best? Forget that, how about my first time at a Jay-Z and Kanye West concert? Up to this day, no words can ever do justice to describe my emotional state at those events. I was beyond star-struck. My state of mind was elevated even further when my friends and I took a road trip to Miami, then to the Port of Miami to disembark in the Bahamas. I was mind blown and motivated at the same time. I got a major energy boost! There was so much out there to enjoy … for those who have the financial resources and time.

After completing my master's degree, I was fortunate enough to secure a high-paying management job with a private healthcare company. It was here that I met a man who greatly influenced my life: the company director. A former military man, he was strict to the point that employees would approach me to air their concerns. Surprisingly, we got along well, and I soon discovered that his 'scary' face was just a façade. He ended up becoming my professional coach, and he always reminded me to talk less and let my work speak for itself. Unfortunately, all he could offer me was professional wisdom, not a work visa – and that was critical to my breakthrough in the land of the free.

After several consultations with my employer about the potential of sponsoring me to obtain a work visa, I had to move on against both my own will and that of the company. The work visa lottery was not in our favour.

I re-enrolled in college, this time a technical college for a hands-on skilled trade, hoping to be more competitive once I was back on the market. "Dude, just get married to your girlfriend," friends kept insisting. I just wasn't ready for this ginormous step; there was so much out there I aspired to achieve. Most of my international friends had taken this step. While they had solved their immigration issues, they had traded their peace of mind. Some opted to study further in anticipation that Obama's government would have an immigration overhaul in favour of international students. Others returned to their respective home countries against their will. The rest opted either to be illegal immigrants, performing odd jobs that paid under the counter or to seek asylum.

The journey to emancipation came with unexpected hurdles. While attempting to focus on my homework one night, I heard gunshots downstairs. Straightaway, I locked my door and wrote a note that included my next of kin's contact information and a love message to my mother and siblings. After 6 hours on lockdown, I learned that I was living with a drug dealer, an ex-convict, and a woman 'they' claimed was a prostitute. No wonder there was always chaos in that house! Even the landlord would sometimes have to wait a few extra months because he'd simply be told the rent wasn't there. The human being is certainly an actor; never in my wildest imagination would I have ever thought such was the case. My roommates were respectful, and frequently we'd go out together for pizza. Perhaps I should have put on my Sherlock Holmes cap more often!

Upon narrating my ordeal to a tutor, he immediately summoned me to vacate the ghetto and seek refuge in Utopia – his home. A renowned Doctor of Philosophy, he was blessed with abundant philosophical knowledge, and he played a critical role in shaping me to be the man I am today.

During my studies at college, one of my siblings who had constantly heard me narrate my escapades decided it was time to face the elephant in the room. I mean, how long was I going to be on these student visas, pumping money into the system? She sent me an email with information about a one-year graduate program in Australia. We agreed it was going to be my last shot at this visa lottery before packing a 23kg suitcase and a 7kg carry-on case back to the motherland. She took a chance on me!

I sold my car, possessions, and stored my valuables in my professor friend's attic. I was granted permission to complete my studies in Australia because I only had one semester left. Once again, I had to pack a decade of my second life into a suitcase, this time to Australia. I was wiser and more determined to become the best I could be. Bittersweet as it was, I had to move on. My friends could not believe I was taking this leap of faith. All I got from my Professor roommate were blessings. His parting words were: "Don't forget me when you make it."

Adapting to the Australian 'desert climate' was probably my toughest challenge; everything else, particularly on the academic front, was under control. Before I knew it, the universe had strategically aligned me with the right people, and it seemed I was in the right place at the right time. For at least a year, I worked as a kitchen hand in a hippy restaurant where I earned minimum wage. Who cares if you are the most educated personnel, qualified to manage the restaurant? As my mother always reminded us when we were young, "Stay humble, and the Almighty will exalt you." I was in a good place and highly optimistic about life again. My colleagues always wondered what my story was; I probably would have wondered the same thing if I were in their shoes. Here was a black guy with an American accent, washing dishes. Couldn't he just become a rapper or a basketball player like the rest of them? Besides, why would he even leave America and come to Australia? It is certainly better to keep them guessing while you are making silent power moves, then before they know it, you are on national TV, and they wonder how you made it there!

Even though it has taken me several years to finally figure out my niche, every morning when I meditate, I thank the universe that I never gave up or even considered adopting a carefree attitude and negative perspective on life. At this stage in my life, I am comfortable and at peace with the universe, though not yet where I am destined to be. If Donald Trump can be the president of the 'most powerful' nation on the planet, the sky must be the limit!

8

Home Will Always Be Home

I migrated from Zimbabwe at the young age of nineteen years to come to the United Kingdom to study nursing. Luckily, I had managed to secure a place at a university in the UK while I was in Zimbabwe with the help of my cousin who was already residing there.

As I was growing up in Zimbabwe, I never envisioned myself going to the UK. In fact, it was all by chance that I ended up migrating. I thank my kind and caring auntie who saw potential in me and asked me if I would consider studying nursing. I had just finished my A-Levels and had plans to go to university in Zimbabwe and study food technology. But it was unclear whether this would actually happen. It was right at the time when the Zimbabwean dollar was starting to freefall and lose its value, and Zimbabwe was going through a land reformation, all of which led to hyperinflation in the years that followed. Therefore, migrating seemed like a reasonable idea.

My family were so poor that they could not afford to pay for my flight to England. My uncle paid for my return ticket, saying that I had to pay him back once I started working, which I did. I'm grateful to such angels who appeared in my life at the right time of need. I can remember the day I arrived at Heathrow airport. My auntie and my cousin were waiting for me. I did not have any problems with immigration; they gave me a one-year visa straight away as I had my letter of acceptance from the university and my accommodation had already been arranged. I also had a bursary allowance in place towards my upkeep, so the immigration officers did not give me a hard time.

I stayed with my cousin for two weeks and managed to get some university paraphernalia before starting my studies, and my cousin told me all about the dos and don'ts of the British culture from her experience.

Shortly after I arrived in the UK, we met my cousin's work colleague for lunch. Just as we were about to eat, we were interrupted by the BBC news. Immediately, we saw the catastrophic events that unfolded on the 11th day of September at the New York City twin towers in the United States of America. That day will be etched on my heart forever. I felt such sorrow, helplessness, sadness and grief, even though none of my family members was involved. None of us could help as we watched innocent people lose their lives. One can ask why someone had the audacity to carry out such an atrocity. At what gain would someone do such acts to destroy others' lives and one's own? One can only be left without words. May those innocent people who died rest in peace.

I started university in mid-September and lived in a flat sharing with six European girls. It was interesting living in the same house and sharing a kitchen and bathroom. I was shocked by their behaviour; they used to go out almost every weekend, and some would bring their boyfriends to their rooms for sleepovers. I had never been out clubbing in my home country. Therefore, I was reserved and kept myself to myself.

Luckily, none of them got pregnant; I am sure they were well stocked up with contraception, which was foreign to me. I always refused to go out with them, even to a movie. I guess this was due to my upbringing. Whether it was good for me or not, it seemed OK at the time. Now, I feel it is a shame that I did not bond well with them and that I have not been able to keep in touch with any of them. It would have been nice to see where they are now and what they are up to, but I guess what's meant to be will be.

I had to learn fast how to transition to this cold country, as I used to call it. I remember that during my first year in the UK, I had to keep the central heating on all the time, even in summer, because I was so cold. I missed home a lot and called my family a lot, but as time progressed, life just moved on. Zimbabwe ceased to be my home and became a place I went to on holiday. I still miss the joy, laughter and family union we used to have on an almost daily basis. Despite being poor, we were very happy in our poverty, simply living each day as it came.

I qualified as a nurse three years later. By then, I had passed my driving test and bought myself a small little run around car, which came in handy for work – it meant I didn't have to wait for a long time to get a bus in the bad weather. I also had the freedom to travel and meet friends in others parts of the UK. That same year, I met the man who became my boyfriend and then my husband a few years later. We got married in a Church of England church, surrounded by friends and family. We celebrated with a meal in an all-you-can-eat restaurant. It turned out to be a great day despite our skinny budget (we spent a small amount for the whole day). All we wanted was to be married and be together, which we still are, now nearing our 10th anniversary. Hopefully, we'll soon be starting a family, too!

It was amazing how ignorant some British people were about Africans. Some thought that coming from Africa meant that we were uncivilised, that Africans lived with monkeys in the trees and, of course, that we were extremely poor. Some British people even believed that they were superior and more advanced to Africans because they were more civilised. And some would comment that we were lucky to be in the UK, living in a civilised country instead of living with the monkeys in trees in Africa! Oh, how ignorant they were! If only they knew that because they colonised us a century ago, we spoke their language even better than some of them did! Not only that, but Africans don't live in trees – we never have! Plenty of Africans live in comfortable houses, bigger and better than the houses in the UK. Saying that, many thanks go to the British for coming to change our ways of life, including our diets. It's not that what we had a century ago was bad … it was just different. Sometimes, I wished I could take the British with me on holiday so that they could see with their own eyes the vast and spacious land of Zimbabwe: the greenery, the beautiful first-class service we provide in our hotels, the lovely warm sunshine, the expansive real-life zoo aka safari, and the magnificent Victoria Falls. I am sure they would be speechless and would start respecting the people of African origin, as they are potentially better in some things.

It makes me wonder what my life would have been like if I had stayed in my home country. Where would I be now? What career would I have picked? I feel that nursing was not my choice – it was coincidental and made economic sense – my circumstances chose it for me. As for my friends who stayed in Zimbabwe, some are doing well and some not so well. Most of them, however, have had to innovate and adapt to run their own businesses and to make it in Zimbabwe. They have managed to adapt to the changes in hyperinflation and the introduction of the bond note. I am sure that in this kind of situation, one has to adapt; there is no choice. It's more like the survival of the fittest – either you evolve with the changes or succumb to the inevitable death that awaits.

Living in the United Kingdom is not what it's made out to be. You can succeed, and you can fail. Someone who comes from a life of poverty in Africa to become a nurse in the UK will live hand to mouth, I am sorry to say, as it only pays enough for a person to survive for one month. If that's all a person aspires to, they will remain on that treadmill until they retire. It's modern economics, I guess. If a person is paid too much, they will not want to return to work the next day. If you desire more than the basics of raising a family, paying your rent or mortgage, and having a holiday once or twice a year, then you have to think outside of the box. One has to be versatile and astute in the administration and management of their financial affairs.

I have even considered migrating to the Middle East, Australia or the USA where nurses' wages are better than the UK, but one thing is for sure … if you have not mastered the creation of wealth, you will spend the rest of life chasing after your pay cheque. Since one cannot keep chasing after money for a stable life, will I end up globetrotting for a pay cheque? Some are doing well in this country, so what are they doing differently to me? I am sure there are better ways, more ingenious ways to improve oneself and circumstances.

Nevertheless, people in Zimbabwe think I am the Bank of England. Basically, I print money whenever they need emergency cash! At least, that's the way they treated me. Maybe it was my fault because I was kind enough to be there for everything they needed. Maybe they got used to begging me for help, instead of using their own initiative or getting a job to earn money for themselves. I had to learn the hard way. And I had to let them know (indirectly) that money does not grow on trees in the UK. I have to work and sweat to make a living, why can't they do the same? Whenever I told them I didn't have money, the next day they would ask again using a different angle, perhaps getting someone else to ask. But the more I stood my ground, the fewer the requests for money came, and I wonder how they started managing by themselves. I guess, sometimes, it was my own fault. I felt guilty about being in England and having a better life than they did, so I felt I should oblige all the time and send money whenever a need arose. But Selah!! Enough is enough. We were all given hands and legs and, therefore, we must put them to good use by providing for ourselves and not depending on others.

Looking back on my life, I am glad about the way it panned out. I have learnt a lot. I have met so many good people in the world, and I am not so sure if I would have survived the challenges that my people in Zimbabwe went through. But there is hope in the air! With a new president, we hope for a better future for Zimbabwe ... or is it just a continuation of the old regime hidden under the sheep's coat? Only time will tell.

I don't regret having the opportunity to live in diaspora. I am grateful to have had the opportunity, but I still miss the lovely proper warm summer weather of Zimbabwe and the winters with NO SNOW. I certainly do not see myself spending the rest of my life in the UK. Home will always be home. My heart will always be in the place where I was born. I have lived in the UK for almost half of my life, and I have adjusted to many of the good things: having electricity day in and day out, the easy access to amenities, the ability to travel around the world, receiving my pay cheque on time, the stable systematic way of living, and the stable economy (until Brexit). But home will always be home: the purity of the land, spending quality time with loved ones uninterrupted by a shift, and the serenity and peacefulness of nature where you can hear birds chirping in the trees all day long.

If I were to live again, I would certainly consider migrating or travelling during the early part of my life, like European students who take gap years to see the world. I would definitely travel, but I probably wouldn't stay in one place for such a long time. Sometimes, I feel like life is passing by so fast that I can't get hold

73

of it. Days are flying by so fast that I wonder if this is it … if all we have to do is coast along until retirement and death. Although, I can say the future looks bright. I can say that having had this time to reflect. The future can only be bright, as one must learn from their follies and find ways to make tomorrow a better day. Otherwise, one ends up repeating them. As for those considering to migrate, each day is what you make it be. I would say: go for it with an open mind. For me, home will always be home!

9

Never Give up on
Your Hopes and Dreams

———————

Having finished high school and worked in a bank for a while, I decided that it was time I sought 'greener pastures' … as I called them. Migrating was the thing to do at the time in Zimbabwe since bad economic times were beginning to show. My sister thought it was a good idea for me to go to America, so we went through the process of obtaining a visa. Everything went well until the family I had arranged to stay with changed their minds about me living with them, which meant I had nowhere to stay when I arrived! Hence, the plan changed. Instead of America, I was going to England. My sister's friend, named Annie, had agreed to accommodate me.

I remember very well the day before I travelled to the UK – I sat with my family while they all wished me well. They were optimistic for my life overseas. I left Zimbabwe at night and arrived in England the following morning with great excitement and great anxiety of what was to come. There were no issues at the airport as I had come to visit and had my American visa with the intention of proceeding to the US. I had to make my own way to the place where I would be staying since Annie was at work and wasn't able to pick me up. Sitting in the coach on my way to London Victoria station, I thought to myself, "Is this really me in London?" From the station, I travelled to the town where Annie lived, then took a taxi to her house.

I was quite amazed at how big Annie's house was on the inside, as it didn't look that big from the outside. A housemate took me to a room that was right at the top of the house and told me it was Annie's room. When Annie returned from work that evening, she showed me the whole house. She also told me that we had nothing to do with the rest of the house and that our sole space was that box room, which could only fit a small bed. We shared other facilities, such as the kitchen and bathroom, with the other people who lived in the house. Well, that was not what I expected to find in England! I thought everyone lived in mansions! My greatest shock was when she told me how we were going to be living. She informed me that she worked every night and that I would be working during the day so that I could sleep on the bed at night and she could use the bed during the day!

I didn't mind working every day as I wanted to earn some money to send to my family back home. Annie helped me find a job in a nursing home. From then on, we would go for days without seeing each other.

Annie was also from Zimbabwe, and after a while, she decided to return home to her family. As I started to accumulate money, I decided to look for a better place to stay. Annie's cousins lived in the same area, and they leased me a room that was slightly bigger than the loft room Annie and I had shared. Later, I moved to a bed-sit, sharing with Annie's sister who had come from Zimbabwe. Life seemed OK. We had a place to stay, and we had lined up a few jobs for ourselves, which included care work and cleaning. I remember too well one of our jobs, which was cleaning the fridges and freezers at a supermarket. We started at 4:00am every day, except Sundays, even in the winter!

As someone who enjoyed studying, I wanted to pursue a career, so I applied for nurse training. I was called for an interview at a university that I could not even remember applying to, and that was where I ended up doing my training! This required me to move to a new city, and I was given accommodation on the university's campus. I met some other students who were also from Zimbabwe. As much as there was studying to do, we always made time to play as well! I recall those three years as a happy and exciting time of my life in England.

One gloomy day, a letter came in the post about the renewal of my visa. It said that my application to extend it had been refused because my lawyer submitted it late. When I tried to contact the lawyer, I was informed that the practice was no longer available and there was nothing I could do to extend my visa. I was then invited for an interview at the Home Office, but that resulted in me being detained and sent to a detention centre. I wondered what I had done wrong and started to worry that I was going to be deported. I did my best to keep my hopes and dreams alive, and this is what enabled me to survive in the detention centre. I was released a week later on two conditions: that I signed into the police station every week, and that I didn't travel outside of the city where I was studying. I was happy to be released and return to university, but even then, I always felt like a prisoner because I could not travel. Every time I saw someone packing to travel to Zimbabwe or heard someone talking about visiting Zimbabwe, my heart would break, as I knew that it was something I could not do. I did not know whether I would ever see my family again. The struggle to have my visa extended continued but, thankfully, the university allowed me to continue with my studies while I tried to sort it out.

I consulted another lawyer who applied for a different type of visa for me. It was a Wednesday afternoon when I went to this lawyer's office, and he told me that my visa had been refused and that my case was hopeless. He said that no one could do anything for me, and he warned me that anyone who said otherwise would be lying. I left feeling very deflated. I thought this was it for my life in England, and I wondered if should go back to Zimbabwe.

I had finished my nurse training, but no one could employ me as a qualified nurse as they needed to see my visa status. I left the city where I had studied and moved around a little bit, managing to get a few small jobs to sustain myself. Sometimes, I felt like throwing in the towel, as I was quite depressed and hopeless about my situation. At one point, I was living in constant fear that I would be deported. I am forever grateful to friends who helped me along the way, and I clung to my faith, which kept me going. Throughout all of these struggles, I believed God was working things out for me, but I also knew that I had to do something.

One of my friends advised me to apply for a nursing job in Ireland. At that time, I did not know where Ireland was, but I was willing to give it a go. I was invited for an interview in

Ireland, but when I tried to get there, I was sent back to England. I was told that I needed to have a status in England in order to travel to Ireland. My hopes were shattered once again, but where there is a will, there is a way. The hospital in Ireland arranged to do telephone interviews with me, and other hospital interviewers travelled to England to interview me! I got a job in Ireland, and when all the paperwork was done, I moved to my new home in a new country.

To me, Ireland was a land of opportunities. It was a chance for a new start, to rebuild my life and hopes once again. There were some ups and downs but nothing that I could not handle. I felt a sense of freedom, and the following year I visited my family in Zimbabwe whom I had not seen for about 8 years. I can truly say that the reunion was quite emotional! While in England, I had lost hope of ever seeing my family or even visiting Zimbabwe, unless I had been deported or decided to leave it all and go back for good. I am grateful to God that through all these challenges, He kept my family safe and I was able to see them all alive when I went home that first time. I have my own family now in Ireland, and I am truly grateful for that. Things are definitely looking up for us. I'm working as a nurse and advancing in my career, which has given me so much pleasure. Also, I'm free to travel anywhere in the world and even embark on different projects without limits. The test definitely became the testimony. Never give up on your hopes and dreams.

10

Of the Home Concept and Such

That moment, that single solitary moment when I presented my passport, driving licence and credit card to the car rental company and noticed that they were all from different countries, is the moment I realised that I was truly living in diaspora. The confused look on the agent's face amused my newly enlightened diasporan self and confirmed what I was beginning to realise.

Where is home? Where am I from? Am I still from there? Will I ever go back there? These questions flashed through my mind, and as my equally confused shared-moment-counterpart was about to blurt out the inevitable, "Where are you from?" question, I promptly shut it down by nonchalantly stating that it was a long story. Actually, I was rather hungry (read: borderline hungry) and did not want to launch into tales of my past with this perfect stranger that was not my (imaginary) psychiatrist. As I was about to drive away, I paused for a long moment as thoughts of home flooded my jetlagged mind, and I wondered again where home really was. Home seemed more of a concept, given that the past nineteen years of my life had been spent outside of my country of birth, Zimbabwe, and I had left when I was nineteen years old. This year would mark living outside of my home country for half of my life, so no thanks to the confused car rental agent, that question plagued me even more: where is home?

In conversation, when I say I am going home, I could mean one of five countries. Home could be Zimbabwe where I was born and raised. Home could be Canada where I spent eight years in higher education. Home could be England where my mother lives. Home could be the Netherlands where I own a house. Home could be Singapore where I currently work. Home could be somewhere else that my future path could take me. As such, when I am engaged in conversation, one may have to pry a little more for details when I mention anything about (the concept of) home. A habit of mine is not volunteering information or giving any details unless asked specific questions.

To backtrack umpteen odd years, I left Zimbabwe to fulfil my higher education endeavours. With my mother and brother already living in diaspora in England and Scotland, respectively, I intended to join them in the United Kingdom. After a series of unexpected events, I was informed by personnel of the Universities and Colleges Admissions Service (UCAS) that they had experienced a system error with my application and that I would need to reapply the following year. What they were really saying (but could not own up to) was that they had received it but didn't know what they had done with it (read: they lost it), and consequently, they did not send it out to my chosen universities (due to its permanently lost state). By sheer dumb luck, I had applied to a few universities in Canada and was accepted by one a few weeks later. As intended, I did leave Zimbabwe for my higher education, but my diaspora path led me to Canada instead of the United Kingdom.

As far as I knew, Canada was a cold, cold, cold place in North America. Why people would choose to live in such a place was beyond me, and then it dawned on me that I was about to live there too! My tropical blood was ready for the inevitable war with the cold country. Upon landing in mid-August, armed with the best thick 'winter' jacket one could buy in Zimbabwe, I found myself sweltering in an intense heatwave that shocked my unprepared senses into a sweating fiesta of sorts. It seems the brochures about Canada did not mention that mid-August was usually accompanied by a scorching heatwave, and the corduroys I was sporting at the time were not aiding in any cooling down process whatsoever. Going through immigration with a 'green bomba' (read: Zimbabwean passport) is a stressful enough experience, yet there I was, perspiring profusely, as I approached the immigration officer ... this was clearly about to be an international immigration incident that would make the evening news. The cheeky immigration officer casually mentioned that they apparently did not tell me in Zimbabwe that August was excessively warm. I did not dare correct him to say that it was not *apparently* but *evidently obvious* their brochures omitted that juicy nugget of information given my current sweaty-mess state.

Divine intervention allowed me and my sweaty self to cruise past immigration with only the usual twenty questions all immigrants receive. En route to my temporary pre-university residence, it sank in that I was the only member of my immediate and extended family in North America. I was nineteen, alone, with two suitcases to my name, half a semester's tuition fees in my pocket, and halfway across the world in a foreign country that was hot. It did not take long to notice that I was no longer a member of the majority. Having grown up in a predominantly black Zimbabwean environment, settling into a place where I was now a visible minority would take some adjusting to. I viewed this new (soon to be incessant) experience as an extension of my boarding school experience back in Zimbabwe, minus the big metal trunk filled with food, name tags on all my clothing and going home every three to four weeks. I would be in Canada for a while.

I swiftly adapted to my new surroundings, and my new place of residence felt strangely like home due to the company I kept. My university flatmate came from Kenya, and my upstairs neighbours were from Morocco. Through them, I befriended others from Ghana, Zimbabwe and other corners of the sub-Saharan continent. Having these close African friends allowed me to not feel so isolated from my southern African roots and elevated my Canadian experience as a diasporan.

I found the city to be a decidedly diverse melting pot of cultures and very accepting of foreigners. This, of course, was within the university campus bubble. Once out of the campus bubble, I sadly did experience some real aspects of the city, such as being racially profiled by the police on more than one occasion. Walking home 'while being black' in a middle-class neighbourhood was apparently one of my off-campus offences. On campus, my Zimbabwean origins were something of a curiosity to my fellow classmates. To non-diasporans, I talked differently, I walked differently, I viewed things differently, and I even ate differently to the tune of not considering a plate of food without meat in it as a full meal … Africans! To this day, one is still hard-pressed to find an African who is a vegetarian. This university campus was multinational and multicultural, but those of African origins were rather a select few. Strangely, my cultural identity grew stronger even with the minimal on- and off-campus dose of African influences, as I realised again that I was now, for the first time in my life, a visible minority.

The visible minority feel escalated further when I moved to the Netherlands and lived among the Dutch. With the Dutch language sounding similar to Afrikaans, a sense of being at home in the Netherlands made it a relatively welcoming place. The exceptionally tall locals were a delight, the ever-present guttural 'g' was a mouthful and then some, and the insatiable appetite for a *bara kip* and *roti kip* threatened to keep me fat and giggly in Dutchland for years to come. My first experience of the Netherlands was in Amsterdam, and this is where I felt like Wesley Snipes in a bowl of rice! Initially, I did not think I could last long in a place like this. To my delight, though, upon going to my chosen city to dwell in, I perceived that it contained a vast collection of people of many races, many mixed races and many people of colour. None from Zimbabwe, however.

When my curious self would ask the locals about their origins, many would say that they were originally from elsewhere but ended up in the Netherlands due to their parents moving or because they themselves immigrated or swam in from somewhere. When asked the same thing, I found I would (and still) say that I am not *originally from* Zimbabwe, but I am *still from* Zimbabwe. An internal conundrum had begun to brew within me, though. The Netherlands quickly became home despite the fact that I still called Canada home, and here I was saying that I was *still from* Zimbabwe! The years rolled by, and after many a *kapsalon*, whenever I was in a slightly inebriated state en route home (read: biking home drunk), I would wonder where home really was … was it just becoming a concept? Curiously enough, those in an inebriated state of sorts always seem to find their way home from a night out on the town. Would I, one day, end up back in Harare after a night out…?

I discovered that to belong to a place, one must blend in with the locals. In the case of the Netherlands, I had to learn the guttural 'g' to really blend in. I noticed that most Dutch are fluently bilingual, so learning their language made it difficult as they automatically switched to English as soon as they heard me butcher their language. I recall a time when I visited home (Zimbabwe) and began speaking in my native tongue when conversing with the kombi driver en route to town. When the driver (and his trusty *hwindi*) both switched to English to converse with me, I was somewhat taken aback. Rude?! Even ruder was the fact that I was charged tourist prices! If my own people could tell I had been away for a while, and I didn't sound or look like I was from Zimbabwe, was Zimbabwe still my home? It was yet another newly enlightened diasporan moment.

This 'concept of home' issue plagued me for months and years to come following this enlightening occurrence. Incidentally, after a series of life-changing events, I decided to make home wherever I was, and thus, I bought my first home in the Netherlands. Family came to visit me, and family came to live with me. My walls were decorated (and still are) with paraphernalia from Zimbabwe and other corners of the African continent. Home had now become within these four walls in Europe. Home was also still my beloved Canada. Home was, and always will be, Harare, Zimbabwe. It dawned upon me that (the concept of) home is where you make it. I planned to live in the Netherlands indefinitely, but as we God-fearing people know, He sometimes has other plans for us. As my permanently-residing-in-Dutchland plans derailed, I quickly accepted the fact that my diasporan antics were going to lead me to yet another culture. As such, I left my homey four walls in the Netherlands and wound up in south-east Asia on the little red dot they call Singapore.

The further east I moved, the more I became the visible minority. Singapore is a fantastic place to be, but the lack of people of colour shocked me. I could go for days without seeing 'a brother or sister' anywhere. When I finally did, there was an instant head nod, an enthusiastic wave, or better yet, an instant conversation leading to automatic friendship. Here, I truly felt like I was in diaspora … the *diaS'pore* if you will. Intriguingly, I met more (non-family) Zimbabweans in Singapore than I did during my fifteen years in the Netherlands and Canada combined. Within a few months of being in Singapore, my cultural identity grew exponentially, probably on account of Singapore consisting of all of thirty-eight Africans ... and counting.

Africans and people of colour are still relatively new to Singapore. It took almost six months for my neighbours to start speaking to me. Even then, the conversations centred on questions of whether I lived there or not. Seeing these people daily for more than six months may have tipped them off to the fact that I now lived amongst them. The questions were also studded with interest of the African continent, and some seemed amazed to see people of colour (read: black people) living amongst them in Singapore. Africans and black people seemed to be a recent addition to the multicultural centre that is now Singapore with its four major languages: Chinese (Hokkien), Malay, Tamil and English. At some point in some ambitious future, what African language would they add to this collection? Life in Singapore was a seamless adaptation for me due to the English speaking people everywhere, save for the odd *auntie* or *uncle* who always seemed confused with my pseudo-African accent. Let it be known that at this point, I was multilingual, so deciphering where I was from based on my accent was not an easy task.

As previously mentioned, my cultural identity exploded, and I took comfort in the sub-Saharan sounds that led me to become a DJ in Singapore. To me, this would bring together the African community for a sense of that (concept of) home feeling. In truth, my addiction to music needed to be fed, so I figured: why not do it with African music and share that passion with my fellow Africans who were also calling Singapore home? At the time of putting pen to paper, I still reside in Singapore, and I'm making plans to make Singapore my home. Somehow, though I feel that Singapore will be added to my collection of homes as new paths and new adventures await my now seasoned diasporan self.

Certain questions still rummage through my mind that I'd like to leave with you. The concept of home is a real one that is faced by all of us in diaspora. Are we here because home is not an option for us to do what we do? Will we go home when we have done what we came to do? Or will the new country become our home? Will our future generations raised away from our country of birth identify with that country at all? Will they call it home? Is home where one is from or where one chooses to make a home? If one has been gone from their city and country of birth for x-amount of time and have made a home elsewhere, where then is home? Are we living in an age where (the concept of) home is not a singular entity but could possibly be on every continent on this planet?

11

The Journey to England

Upon my arrival in England, I was really excited and happy to see my sister. I was also looking forward to life in the UK as a twenty-year-old. We got on the tube, and I was mesmerised by how fast this train was moving. We travelled for at least an hour and a half to reach her place. I don't really know what I was expecting, but I was surprised that her accommodation was a small two-bedroom flat that she shared with two other tenants. This meant that the lounge was occupied as well as both of the bedrooms. "My goodness," I thought, "is this England?" I slept that night with mixed emotions of excitement and shock.

I woke up the next day grateful to be in England. My first impression was that it was somewhat quiet; there was not much activity. It seemed that most people went to work in the mornings and returned in the evenings after a long day at work, leaving no time to relax. After a few days, my sister told me that I needed to work so that I could contribute towards the bills. I was a visitor to the country and, therefore, I was not allowed to work, but my sister said she would help me find employment (happy days).

She was glad, at least, that we could start sharing the bills. I secured employment at a college via a catering agency, and my job entailed making sandwiches. My sister showed me the route I needed to take to get to the college, and I started work.

I worked for two weeks before getting my first pay cheque, and it was a measly £110! "What?" I despaired. The amount didn't seem to justify the many days of waking up at 5:00am to commute, then getting home at 7:00pm. Wow, this was hard. On top of that, seeing other young people at the college gave me low self-esteem. I was not daft, and I wanted to study law, so why wasn't I enrolled in a university? "Well, you are an international student, and fees are high. Forget that law degree, you can't afford it," my sister told me. My sister informed me how she had extended her visitor's visa by enrolling at a college, which was cheaper than studying at university. This option gives migrants a one-year visa that can be renewed annually. The other advantage is that students can work legally for 20 hours per week.

Life in the UK was hard. The only joy was going to car boot sales and buying clothes for 50p. I was vain, so it was painful to be this low in life. Anyway, after a little while, I bought myself a mobile phone, and that was my greatest achievement that year. I was always broke; the bills seemed endless, and my travel card had to be topped up every week. It was a never-ending nightmare. I became really depressed and lost all self-esteem. I also started smoking cigarettes and drinking alcohol as a way of fitting in. The only role model I had was my sister, and she spent every God-given minute working or sleeping.

The winter was harsh. Oh, my dear, I did not expect darkness at 3:30pm! When I awoke, it was dark, when I went to work, it was dark, and when I returned home, it was dark … my mood was dark as well. Some of my friends back home had finished their university studies and were in good jobs, and here I was in England, stuck making sandwiches. For someone who did well at school, this felt uncomfortable. I felt life was unfair. My dark hole became worse, and my sister told our family back home that I was not coping well. They recommended I return to Zimbabwe, which suited me, as I really wanted out. I'd had enough of life in England.

I returned to Zimbabwe after a year in the UK. As much as I loved being home, it felt strange … like I didn't belong. I started yearning to be back in that dark and not-so-friendly country called England. Why, though? It was then that I remembered a book I had read during my A-levels about a girl called Tambu and her anglicised cousin, Nyasha. Oh, my God, I was becoming anglicised! I didn't like the hustle and bustle of Zimbabwe, I didn't enjoy travelling in Zimbabwean taxis, and I disliked the loud, uncultured youths who whistled at any female wearing a mini skirt. I wanted out of Zimbabwe again. I was a confused young lady.

"I did nursing when I was your age before I became a dentist," my Aunt said. "England is full of opportunities if you are willing to take them." She suggested I returned and enrolled at a university to study nursing or something related to healthcare.

So, a year later, there I was, twenty-two years old and back in England trying out a new life. With the help of my sister, I was fortunate enough to get a university place to study nursing, and I completed my three years with the help of a bursary. Student life was not that easy, especially because there was always someone back home waiting to be fed or someone's child waiting for their school fees to be paid. It meant that instead of working just 20 hours, I was working a lot more hours than I was permitted, or was wise. Also, trying to adjust to the curriculum and learning ICT (Information Communication Technology) skills was not easy, but I was determined. Nursing was the key to my future.

I lived at the nurses' residence for the first year of my studies and then moved to private shared accommodation for the remaining two years. I graduated three years later, and I've worked as a nurse ever since. My first job was at an old psychiatric hospital. I didn't enjoy it … not because I didn't love what I did, but because this type of medical care had a negative effect on my emotional wellbeing.

I got into a relationship with a colleague. He was charming, but I later found out that he was already married. One thing is for sure – relationships in England are hard! You meet either the ones who are already taken or the ones who pull you down because they are graduates in lies and manipulation. Several years later, I got pregnant and gave birth to a beautiful daughter. I've found it difficult to have a relationship in England, especially with Africans who can't cope with the fact that female roles have changed. For example, some men from Africa expect women to go to work all day, then do all the chores when they come home, such as cooking, cleaning, serving the food, washing up, washing the clothes and ironing. I was too independent. Why should I come home after a long day at work to cook for a man who spends his day flicking the remote at home? I tell you, some African guys in England do this a lot. They find a woman who works hard and who can look after them, then they buy her designer clothes. Their attitude is, "What more will the woman want?" Well, I wasn't going to put up with that in my life. I was better off single than being miserable looking after a grown man.

I worked hard at my job and managed to secure promotions. I am proud of myself. The opportunities are out there; however, for Africans, those opportunities do not come easy. If you want to succeed, you have to work hard. You have to go the extra mile to be recognised. I don't think it's due to racism; it's institutional habits that have been created because black people don't seek the opportunities for fear of being rejected. Instead, black people sit back and are content. I have always been ambitious for career progression, so I have challenged myself to go for what I want. I have been doing that for years, which has prompted some recognition from my employers.

I chose a different path of not being content with the substandard. I grabbed opportunities by the horns. I fell, but I lifted myself up, and I never gave up or gave in. At the age of thirty, I purchased my first property – a two-bedroom mid-terrace house, which is sufficient for me and my daughter. In hindsight, I believe I am lucky, I was lucky, and I will always be lucky, as the opportunity I was given has shaped my life and will shape the future of my child.

12

Money Does Not Grow on Trees in the UK!

I was born in Harare, Zimbabwe. I did all of my education in Harare. I now live in the United Kingdom. I have two siblings who also live in the UK, and my husband has three siblings in the UK as well.

When I got married, I had to go and live in a remote area of Zimbabwe where my husband was working. He held a good position in the company he worked for, and he was well paid. I also had a job, but my salary was nothing compared to my husband's. Life was not easy for me, as I was very lonely. I spent long periods of time on my own. I had no neighbours to talk to. In fact, I did not trust most of the women in that area because they would smile at me while having another secret mission, which was to get close to my husband with the intention of destroying our marriage.

My married life was not at all a good one. I used to cry day and night. I skipped work and even got to the point of taking an overdose of antidepressants. I then decided that if we could go to another country far from Zimbabwe, life would be better. I didn't want to let my marriage just die without trying to save it.

Initially, I went to the UK on my own. I wanted to find out what it would be like to live there, and I wanted to see if I could pave a way for my husband and daughter to join me. My daughter was two-years-old at the time. When I left, my husband took her to my parents and his parents who were in Harare.

A friend assisted me to get accommodation in a shared house, and I had a little bedroom to myself. I thought I would find work easily, but it did not happen. My friend then contacted the agency she was working for, and I was given a few shifts. I did different jobs: cleaned toilets, worked in a nursing home as a healthcare assistant, and worked in the laundry room of a hospital. I wasn't paid for two weeks, and there were some days when I went to bed on an empty stomach. I had never experienced that before.

In those days, you could buy a tin of baked beans for 20 pence. I would walk along the streets scanning the ground for some money to pick up. There was a day when a Chinese girl approached me and pointed to my trainers. She was showing me that they were falling apart. I had left Zimbabwe with only two pairs of footwear, as I had been advised that after landing in the UK, I could go to a place where tons and tons of designer wear were being thrown away, and I could collect whatever I needed. The question is … has anyone seen such a place since coming to the UK?

After three months, I saw an advert for a credit card in a newspaper that was about to be thrown away by a resident of the nursing home where I was cleaning. I took the application form, completed it and posted it on my way home – the postage was free. When I got home, I told my distant relative who had invited me to stay with her. She said that what I had done was illegal and that the Home Office and the police would be contacted. I did not sleep all night! At the same time, I felt so bad that I was going to expose her to the Home Office. A week went by without the Home Office or the police turning up, but what I received in the post was a credit card with a good amount of credit. I used the little savings I had plus the credit on the card to do some shopping and to return to Zimbabwe. I was not prepared to continue with the kind of life I had found in the UK. I was also missing my daughter.

When I arrived in Zimbabwe, I was distraught to find out that my husband had already taken in another woman, thinking I had gone forever. However, he ditched her upon my return. It so happened that he then lost his job and decided we should go to the UK together. The thought of going back to the UK to look after the elderly and assist them with going to the toilet was a big 'No' for me. But my sister convinced me, saying that if I didn't go, I was not supporting my husband who was in a bad situation in Zimbabwe. My husband wanted us to leave our daughter behind, but I told him I wasn't going anywhere without her.

When we arrived in the UK, we stayed with my sister and her friend for a while. My husband managed to get a job the very week we arrived, but it took me almost six weeks to find employment, and when I did, I worked night shifts. We then rented a one-bedroom flat. We had no furniture, so during the day, when my husband was at work, I walked around the streets looking for furniture that was being thrown away, and my husband would pick it up when he got back from work. We furnished our little place that way.

I applied to study nursing, and when I got a place, my passport, as well as my 6-month visa, had only a few days left before expiring. The university gave me a letter to support my application for a student visa. I was only able to apply for myself and my daughter; my husband's passport had been lost.

I woke up in the early hours to go and queue at the immigration centre in Croydon. Thank God, a dear friend had advised me to get there early. The immigration officer I saw was not that friendly, or maybe she was too keen or thorough in her job. She told me that the university letter did not meet certain standards. Yet, other students had managed to get a visa with the same type of letter. She also pointed out that my passport was expiring and said that she would not be happy putting a visa in a passport that had less than a week to expire. I called the university and spoke to a man who agreed to amend the letter for me, but the immigration officer wanted all the documents to be hard copies, so I had to collect the letter from the university. I honestly don't know how I made it to the university and back to Croydon! When I got off the train, just a few minutes were remaining before the Home Office closed. I ran like a mad person.

The security guard at the door could see me running as he held the door ready to lock it, and he gave me a sign to say, "Run!" When I reached the entrance, I thought I would pass out! I had not had a chance to buy anything to eat or drink due to the hassle I was going through that day. The women who were doing the initial checks and stamping the application forms had already packed the stamps away. They were not happy with the security officer who had let me in the building! But they checked my application and stamped it to say that I had all the required documents. When I arrived at the floor where I had met the lady who refused my application that morning, there were still people waiting. While I was in the queue of about five people, that's when it hit me. I said to myself, "You stand no chance of getting the application approved. What are you doing here?" I comforted myself by thinking, "You never know."

When it came to my turn, the lady put a stamp in my passport and pushed it back to me saying, "Anyway, we share the same birthday," and she closed her counter. I could not believe it! I had been given a student visa for a year, and my daughter had been given a dependent visa. It was that easy.

When I started my nurse training, our situation changed a bit. I was able to work part-time, and I was getting a bursary. Initially, I really did not like nursing, but when I went for a placement in the community, attending to patients in their homes, I enjoyed it. I also liked the 9-5 hours, Monday to Friday and the fact that I didn't wear a uniform. In the second year of my training, my husband decided to do a degree in computer sciences. He was charged the foreign student rates, and it was expensive. He had to self-fund, so he worked extra jobs to cover his fees.

My daughter was quite confused seeing her father going to work in different attires. One of the days when my husband was ready to go to his security job, she asked, "Dad, are you a soldier today?" Another day when he was delivering furniture, and he was wearing a hi-vis, reflective jacket, she asked, "Are you a lollypop lady today?" Then, when he wore a jacket and tie to go for his university placement, she asked, "Are you a teacher today?"

Due to our studies and jobs, we really struggled with childcare. At times, I would bring relatives from Zimbabwe to help, but they would disappear after a week or so … one even disappeared at the airport when she landed! These ladies used me to get into the UK, and I incurred a lot of debt in return.

My husband and I had to own two cars. It was not a luxury; it was a necessity to make it easier for us to get to university and then to work. There were times when I worked nights and my husband worked days that I would meet him in a country lane to hand over our daughter who was already in her pyjamas and sleeping.

After qualifying as a nurse, I wanted to buy a house. To be accepted for a mortgage, I needed to reduce my debts, so I worked three jobs to save money for a deposit. At one point, I worked 28 nights and 20 days consecutively! Finally, I managed to purchase a house.

Coming to the UK has given me the opportunity to see what is on the other side of the world. Whenever anyone in Zimbabwe asks me, "What is it like in the UK?" I tell them exactly what it is like … there is freedom of speech, from the young to the old, the clocks are changed in summer and winter, and some people are friendlier to dogs than to people. But the one thing I am still trying to hammer into the heads of people back home is that money does not grow on trees in the UK – one works hard for it.

I really had a good life growing up in Zimbabwe, but my experience of married life there has really put me off ever going back.

I am comfortable at present. For the past 7 years, I have travelled out of the UK every three months for holidays or business. I no longer work night shifts, as I am building my own business. And the little girl who was tossed to and fro to be looked after while my husband and I were at work is now at university herself.

13

No One Can Ever Take Your Education Away from You

I was born and bred in Harare, Zimbabwe. I attended the top private schools from preschool to high school, and then I was offered a place at a reputable Christian university in Zimbabwe. I gladly went there to study finance, and I started my 'big girl' life away from my parents. I didn't like being so far in the country, but I guess it helped me to focus on my studies ... well, until I met a guy who swept me off my feet.

Being young and mostly naive, we had planned our future together. I firmly believed I would spend the rest of my life with him. Life, however, had different plans for us, and especially for me. He was soon to graduate and return to his country, which neighboured Zimbabwe, and I was to fly across oceans, not knowing what I was to expect in a foreign land.

My second semester was cut short when my father marched onto the university campus and summoning my presence. I was excited to see him, but little did I know that this conversation would change my life forever. I was not asked, but rather told that I was to apply for a US visa and move there for my studies. Any child my age, or even older, may have jumped at this opportunity, but my heart sank, and I realised that my life might not be the exact cookie-cut life that I had planned. I was supposed to get married after my master's degree at twenty-five and have three kids by thirty … but maybe not.

My mother and I applied for the visas, and we were approved. I did not want to believe it, but it was true. I packed my bags, and I was on my way to the USA. I was eighteen, and I had many expectations of what America would be like. I tried to channel my energy to good thoughts of how I would settle in and then send for my boyfriend to join me so that life would not be as miserable as it was promising to be.

Rewind … I am the youngest of four girls. At this point in my life, all of my sisters had migrated. The eldest was married in England, the second was married in the US, and the third was trudging along with school elsewhere in America. I was to stay with the second sister until I could fend for myself. Mum remained in Zimbabwe with my dad; they used their visas to come and visit us from time to time.

I landed in America, and the airport was as I expected: big, busy and scary. I figured my way around after passing through immigration and then borrowed a phone to call my cousin who was picking me up to take me to my new 'home'. I had never met him, so I thought it was going to be awkward, but he made me feel at ease. Driving out of the airport, I saw that the city was crazy! Then we stopped at a nearby McDonald's, and I got a burger and fries. This was my first McDonald's experience, and it was the first for a very long time. I took two bites of the burger and wondered what kind of meat was on my buns. So, I moved to the fries, and they tasted like salted plastic. I sipped on my drink and just waited to get home so that I could, hopefully, eat some better tasting 'real' food.

We drove past a place that smelled like a sewer! And when we finally drew closer to our destination, it was nothing like the San Francisco or Seattle that I was hoping for. Instead, we drove through cornfields, and when we got off the highway, I was hoping we still had some distance to go, but we did not. Oh boy, life just got too real! The house was big and beautiful, but the excitement of being with my sister was drowning, and the reality that I was not in Zimbabwe and probably wouldn't be for a long time was dawning. Days went by, then weeks, and then winter started knocking. I was able to tolerate the cold because I was so excited for the snow to come!

Life got even more real when my sister sat me down to talk about how I was going to survive in America. She told me that I had to have a phone, I had to have a car, I had to go to school, and all of those bills were on me. Hold on, this is not what I signed up for! I had come from a home with the full service – a maid, tuition paid, phone bill paid etc. – only to arrive in the land of milk and honey and be told that I had to make that milk and the honey before I could taste it. Game changer.

I decided to be an au pair while I figured out what to do. Everyone was drilling nursing into my head, and it took me a little over a year to relent. Against my will, I went to nursing school, and I hated every second of my studies. It was only when I experienced nursing first-hand during my first clinical (placement) that I had an epiphany, and my whole perspective changed. I had wanted to continue studying finance with a minor in music, but I looked around and noticed that less than 1% of the people I knew had made it far without a medical background. So, like the typical immigrant parents expected, it was either medicine, engineering or accounting. I was not doing any of those, so I buckled down with my nursing training, hoping to graduate, pay off my loans, go back to school to study finance, and live happily ever after.

I didn't forget about my lost love … he faded away into nothing in under a year, but that was after I heard that he had been cheating on me with his ex and they were expecting a baby. The thing that kept me sane was the knowledge that he wanted to be where I was – in the land of opportunity – but instead, he was a dad out of wedlock, caught cheating and needing to rely on his father for support. Cold, I know, but he got what was coming to him … karma is really true to her calling!

I graduated with honours from nursing school. I met the man I would marry before I even planned on going to school, only to realise that he had migrated just a month after me from Zimbabwe, and we had the same circle of friends. We dated for a long time. We took a breather, and we rekindled the flame. But in the middle of all that, I returned to my studies and qualified as a nursing associate. A year after that, I graduated from university with a bachelor's degree in healthcare management … not finance. The following year, I made the decision to go back to school and fulfil my dream of acquiring my master's degree before the age of thirty. I was accepted and took full-time classes online. I got engaged, married and fell pregnant during the time I was studying! Then I waddled onto the stage eight and half months pregnant to receive my master's diploma, magna cum laude in business administration. I did it! A few weeks later, I fell in love again, but this time it was a love so deep – a love only a mother would understand.

A quick timeline – started my master's degree, started dating my future husband again, got engaged, went back to Zimbabwe for the dowry, got married in under six months, graduated eight months after the wedding, gave birth one month after graduation … and had another baby a year and a half after the first. Talk about fast track! Currently, I am contemplating going back to school to be a nurse practitioner. My husband and I both have great jobs, and we love our beautiful family, but for me, I want to progress even further in my studies. Thankfully, my husband feels the same way, so we will both be students again very soon.

I look back at the whole process of migrating to the US, and it has been miraculous how my path was 'made' because I know of many people who have moved to the US and are still struggling to make their way after fifteen years or more. I am thankful to my dad for seeing where the economy in Zimbabwe was heading and having the intuition to ship me out before I experienced the Great Depression of my home country. I now advise all young people – if they have the interest and the intellect – to go for a medical degree, or any qualification in healthcare. Since I became a nurse, there has never been a time that I have job-hunted for over a few weeks without several job offers. I understand that it is not for everyone, but I did what I had to do at the time, I fell in love with it, and I am pursuing it at an even higher level than I would have ever thought. Forget the job opportunities; it can even help to get someone's status changed, depending on where one works and how badly the company wants the person. I have known several people who have been fortunate enough to have their cake and eat it this way.

My husband and I plan to invest in Zimbabwe. It is inevitable that we will. If the economy was any better, I am sure we would be packed and on our way home. But America has opened so many endless opportunities for us and for our children so we will stay put for a while.

Though I didn't have domestic help when I moved here, I survived. I learned to pick up after myself and be responsible for my actions. I had bills to pay, and no one was going to pay them for me. Credit cards were thrown in my face left, right and centre, and I fell for it and used them ... a lot! I shopped until I had nowhere to put all my 'stuff'. At one point, I had over twelve pairs of shoes. I went crazy with the acquisition of 'things' until I came back to earth and had to decide what I was going to do with my life.

I travelled the world. In four years, I had been to Cape Town twelve times, as well as Kenya, Zambia and Namibia – countries in Africa I did not even visit when I lived in Africa. In those four years, I was blessed enough to also visit Thailand, Hong Kong, Malaysia, Singapore, the UAE, England and Canada. The doors to the world seemed to open from my being in America and that I will never regret. My travel within the US itself has been more extensive than over 90% of the American population, and

I think this is mostly due to my background and the person I have become as a result.

Anyone who knows me knows how important education is to me. I was raised to believe that the only thing that no one can take from you is your education, because it is *yours*, and you gained it through your own sweat and tears. I was raised to never be mediocre, so attaining a B or a C was not the best I could do or be. This played a big role in my first 'failure' when I was at university. I got a C for a class that I really didn't put much work into, but that C tainted my transcript and life for those few years. It is good to have high standards and achieve them, but it is not good if it drags you under the mud when you fail to attain the goals you set for yourself. It is not the failure, but how it's handled and what you do thereafter that matters. From my own lessons, I will encourage my children and other people that an A does not mean you are the best there is. It is a symbol of the work put into it, but it is not what will walk you through the doors of Wall Street to be the cream of the crop. Your character and personality will sell you, and then your grades will back you up. I used to think that if at first you don't succeed, give up and try something else, but life has taught me that where there is a 'reasonable' will, there will always be a way. You just need to open up your eyes and see the path to that destination.

If I were to live all over again, I would realise that I was never in love with the first guy I dated, I would heed the advice of those who have walked on this earth much longer than I have, and I would migrate … even a bit sooner, and start my studies sooner so that I could travel the world much sooner.

I do not regret how it turned out for me, though. I have learned very valuable lessons and made friendships I would never be able to put a price tag on. I have a family I chose for myself, and this is all away from the place I grew up calling home.

14

In Search of Greener Pastures

The clock ticked, and my heart pounded with mixed emotions. It was an extremely hot November day, and I had been told to dress up warm, as my destination would be bitterly cold. But my mind was not on my destination, it was in the present. I was with my husband and our beautiful children, and I was about to leave them to search for greener pastures. I kept checking my ticket, hoping I had the dates wrong. My heart was begging for one more day with my family, but the clock kept ticking, and the time came for me to leave the house and to be escorted to the airport for my flight to the United Kingdom.

I tried my best to be strong. It was the first time I would be apart from my children for more than a few days. "How will they cope?" I worried. "Will they forget me or hate me for leaving them?" Funnily enough, the girls were happy to go to the airport. My husband and son, however, were very sad. The journey seemed long and boring, and I could feel the tension and sadness. Dressed as I was, sweat streamed down my face, masking the tears that also flowed.

This was a real leap of faith; it was a matter of do or die because of the situation in Zimbabwe. I wanted to continue feeding my children and educating them, but our wages remained the same while prices skyrocketed, making the purchase of day-to-day commodities a tough task. We had joined long queues not even knowing what was available to buy until it was our turn. I love my family, so I was not going to watch them be tormented by such hardships. Because of love, I had to brace up and leave my family. As a mother, I had to wear my strong armour and put on my best smile ever, as I knew this was for the good of my children.

I bid my children goodbye, and I can still feel the hugs from the girls (my son refused to come out of the car – he didn't want us to see him cry, especially when the girls appeared to be happy). At the flash of my husband's identity card, we passed through the VIP entrance and then it was just the two of us. We stared at each other. There were no words.

I remembered that my niece from my husband's side of the family was meant to be travelling with me, and that's what broke our silence. Tendai was hoping to join her siblings in the UK. My husband found her and brought her through the VIP entrance. Having Tendai with us made it easier for us to chat, and we even managed to laugh.

When it was time to leave, Tendai and I gave my husband a final hug. I was the first passenger to board the plane, and I didn't look back. Initially, we sat quietly, but Tendai's excitement gave way to conversations about her dreams of gaining an education and purchasing a house. On arrival at Gatwick, a man standing at the main entrance called loudly, "Visitors to this queue and asylum seekers to this queue." I was a visitor, so I joined the appropriate queue. Not long after, Tendai and I showed our documents to the airport staff. My interview was quick and friendly. Tendai's, on the other hand, was terrible – I could hear all the questions she was being asked, and she was struggling to understand what the person was saying. I was frustrated and angry and wanted to answer for her, but I knew that would jeopardise everything. When my interview was over, I was told where to collect my luggage and wished a happy holiday.

The bags rotated round and round. I couldn't remember what my bag looked like. I couldn't think straight. My mind was on Tendai. Had she made it? Finally, I found my bag and left to meet my nephews who were collecting Tendai and my brother who was collecting me.

My brother was not there. One of my nephews phoned him, but the call went unanswered. I took the phone, called again and left a message. I also called his wife and left a message. After an hour of waiting, the disappointing news came that Tendai was being deported. I thought about all her plans and dreams, and her excitement to be with her family – all of it was shattered in an instant. One of her brothers and his wife invited me to their house since there had been no response from my brother. If I had not come with Tendai, I would have been stranded at the airport.

Once outside, I knew the reason why I had been told to dress warmly. It was so cold that I could hardly feel my toes. At my nephew's house, I had a shower but still could not get warm. I rang my husband to tell him I had arrived safely. His voice was hollow. I thought he would celebrate that I had made it, but he just said he'd had a rough night and couldn't sleep. He was already complaining about boredom and wondering how many more nights he would have to go through without me. It was a short call. I was left stunned and speechless. I didn't even speak to the children.

My nephew was surprised that my brother hadn't phoned. We tried phoning both numbers again, but there was still no response. "Strange!" I thought. "Did I get the numbers wrong?" Finally, my brother called and said he was surprised that I had come to the UK without telling him! My jaw dropped. What a welcome! We arranged to meet at 2:00pm the next day at his local train station.

The following day, I boarded a train that would take me to the city where my brother lived. The seats were comfortable, but the high speed made me nervous. I arrived at around 1:00pm, and I stood and waited like a fool until 5:00pm. My stomach was rumbling, I was freezing cold, and my feet were numb. I didn't move an inch, not wanting to miss my brother. Finally, I gave in, as I was desperate to use the toilet. I began to wander around, making sure I wasn't too far away from the station, only to realise there was a McDonald's close by. I used the toilet and hurried to the counters. With the money I had from my nephew, I ordered a hot chocolate. I was surprised by the amount of change I got after the teller kindly asked if I had smaller change. I wasn't familiar with the British currency. I sat down and couldn't wait for the hot drink to cool down, as I was starving and cold.

All of a sudden, I heard an angry voice: "Aunty, you are just sitting here, and I've been looking for you for the past 10 minutes!" No friendly greeting. Nothing. Just complaining about the 10-minute search when I had been waiting in the cold for four hours! But I was so happy to see my brother that I didn't worry about my sister-in-law's anger. That night, there was no cosy bed waiting for me. Instead, my 'bed' was the hallway floor.

Two days later, my sister-in-law gave me a set of house keys, wrote their address on a piece of paper, gave me a map of the city and told me to go and look for work. And that was it. I didn't even have a mobile phone just in case I got lost. I felt let down and frustrated, but I had a mission to accomplish. I walked for an hour that day, just getting familiar with the area. The following day, I managed to catch a bus into town, and I bought myself a mobile phone. Within a week, I had a job as a carer in a nursing home. However, since I was not allowed to work or seek public funds, I had to convince the home to hire me.

I hated everything about the job. Despite wearing gloves when carrying out personal care, I found it difficult to eat with my hands afterwards. Sometimes, while eating, I would have flashbacks of carrying out personal care, and I would be violently sick. I would wash my hands repeatedly with hot water and soap until my skin hurt. It took around six months to settle at work. It didn't come easy, though, as the staff were unfriendly. The only thing that kept me going were the elderly people – they were poorly, but still loving. I was on my feet all day, attending to the residents, even when I was supposed to be on my break. I just didn't want to see anyone distressed.

One morning, after my first ever night shift, I got home and ran the shower, hoping to warm up before eating breakfast and going to sleep. But the water was ice cold, and when I tried to boil the kettle, it didn't work. I was confused, cold and tired, and I went to sleep shaking. I texted my brother and sister-in-law, but I didn't receive a response from either of them. Eventually, my brother responded, saying he was going away for a week and that my sister-in-law would be around to help.

By then, I was on my way to work for another night shift. I left a note to say there was a problem with the power supply, but I didn't see my sister-in-law or hear anything from her during that week. When my bother arrived back, he gave me an inflatable mattress – I had never even known something like it existed! He also explained that their accommodation had a pay-as-you-go meter for electricity, and he took me to the shops and showed me how to buy power. It was evident that my sister-in-law had meant for me to fend for myself. Daily, she had been topping up the meter with just enough money so she could cook a meal and heat herself throughout the night. By morning, there was no power left for me.

Shortly afterwards, we moved to a different part of England. The journey was unpleasant – it was long and cold, we had no satnav, and my brother and his wife bickered throughout. Fortunately, I managed to get a job the following day. I also managed to register at a college for a one-year computer course. This allowed me to gain a student visa. I intended to register for nursing at a later date, but my sister-in-law discouraged me by telling me about her friend who had come to the UK as a visitor and had been deported when she tried to register to train as a nurse. She also told me that I couldn't open a bank account because I would be reported immediately and deported. I cried day and night. And I prayed constantly – my life really depended on it, more than anything else.

I worked at a very posh nursing home. I was the only African carer. The matron called me into her office one day and asked why my salary was being paid into my brother's bank account (he and his wife also worked at the home). Because of the love and care I had shown to the residents, she was interested in me and wanted to help. I opened up and explained my situation, and she wrote a letter to a high street bank. I don't know what she wrote, but she called me into her office again a week later and asked me to go to the bank. On my way, I could hear my sister-in-law's negative words and feel the fear she had instilled in me. I was so afraid, sweating in the cold, as I didn't know if I was doing the right thing. After just one week, I had my bank card! Excitement overtook me, and I felt independent for the first time since arriving in the UK.

As time passed, I worked in other care sectors as an agency carer, and I also enrolled as a student for another college course so that I could renew my student visa. By then, I was working two jobs – one during the day for one employer and another during the night for another employer. I needed to work as much as I could to pay my bills and support my family back in Zimbabwe. Unfortunately, the challenges of living this double life took its toll on me, and I found myself not returning to college. I was too exhausted to cope with my studies, as I ventured further into dangerous ways of living. I would work a night shift then take a taxi to my next job where I would work a long day shift. I lived a life of nonstop work. My wardrobe was in my rucksack – clean underwear, vests, t-shirts and black trousers. I chose t-shirts because they didn't need ironing, and I also took loads of baby wipes for freshening up. I had loved college, don't get me wrong, but at that time, I told myself that I came for 'the money, not education'. Leaving college meant I was fresher for work and the favours from my bosses were flowing in. I found myself getting higher rates of pay than my brother and his wife, but I also accrued many enemies – people disliked me because I worked over and above my call of duty, which made me the manager's favourite. Leaving college also meant that my student visa became invalid, so I applied for asylum. The process took a long time, twelve years in total, during which I continued working. Work was tough, scary at times, but I had to do what I had to do to achieve my goals.

One day, I asked my manager if I could be the one who took a resident to college. I don't know why I volunteered. I was an agency carer, and it was the nursing home's policy that only full-time members of staff could accompany the residents off the premises. However, I was permitted due to the amount of time I worked there each day. At 4:00pm, when college had finished, we waited for our taxi, but it didn't arrive. I rang the manager who said he'd phone for a taxi. He also informed me that the Home Office had visited the care home that day and taken most of the staff to a detention centre because they didn't have the right paperwork to work in the UK. My heart sank low. I was in the same situation. Had I been at the care home that day, I would have been taken away as well. When I got home that night, I prayed like I had never prayed before.

That same week, my brother phoned me while I was at work and told me that our dad had passed away. I refused to believe him and went into denial. At the end of my shift, I went home, and all my friends were there. That's when it began to sink in. I was in deep pain. I blamed myself for being so far away. I wanted to see my father alive; he had been my best friend. I dreaded to think about going home without him being there. And the thought of not being able to attend his funeral broke my heart. I tried to push the pain away by returning to work after only two days.

The employment agency began to hassle me about my Home Office paperwork. They phoned constantly, and one day a lady demanded my National Insurance Number. I told her to have a pen and paper ready, and when she did, I said loudly, "It's J-E-S-U-S!" My colleagues were shocked! Then I said, "I have got work to do. I hope you jotted it down correctly." She responded, "Yes."

Following that, the agency invited me to attend some compulsory training. I rang them two days later to reschedule my training and told them I was going to Zimbabwe for my father's funeral. I changed my sim card, never called them again and started a new job as a cleaner. My friends went to the so-called compulsory training not knowing that immigration officers from the Home Office were in another room. They were asked to complete some paperwork, which was checked immediately, and many of my friends were taken away and deported. It can only be God who saved me, for which I am grateful every day.

I pursued my application for asylum with many immigration lawyers, but all of them just wanted to take advantage of my desperate situation. I lost a lot of money, and others tried to blackmail me into sleeping with them before they processed my papers! These were black Zimbabwean lawyers. Who then could I trust?

Time passed, and I missed many special occasions back home. I missed my eldest daughter's last day at school. I missed my youngest daughter's first day at high school and her first menstrual period. I missed my son's engagement, I missed his wedding and the arrival of my grandchildren. Have I put money before my family? I was sad when my eldest daughter fell pregnant while at university, but her daughter bonded so well with my husband, and that gave me peace. He was kept so busy with our granddaughter that he slowly forgot to ask me that dreaded question, "When are you coming back?"

Yes, there are so many things I have missed. I am blessed, however, that there are so many things I have achieved. I am a breadwinner, and we have never been without. God's hand continues to bless me every day. I managed to educate my children to the end and assist my son in starting a business. I am from a very big family and have helped educate some of my nieces and nephews along the way as well.

My pain does not go unaccounted for: 'No pain, no story'. A life well lived is a life with a purpose, and I believe I was born with the purpose of spreading love everywhere I go. I was born through love and raised in love. Whatever God gives me, I see fit to share with those in need. So, my purpose here on earth is the very reason I am here in diaspora working all kinds of jobs.

My children are grown up now, and when I want to chat, it's as simple as WhatsApp! My son, bless him, is the only one who keeps saying, "Mum, I miss you! Please come back for my sake." My husband changed from being a man who demanded to know when I was coming back to being a man who talks about his grandchildren and how much he loves them. Hey, where is the love?? I am so green with envy. I wish I were there to see them grow up, but it comforts me that he has found a joy that keeps his mind free from being lonely. I still have faith and hope that the Zimbabwe journey will be made pretty soon. As soon as I have saved up enough money for the dream I have to leave a legacy, I will return for good.

15

The Recruitment Process

There was so much excitement to finish my degree because the chances of moving abroad after qualifying as a nurse were high. My friends and I continued to add more and more courses per year, as we needed to polish our profiles to meet the requirements for application. I can remember attending a recruitment seminar where nursing agencies from abroad came to address us about all the requirements needed for the job applications. Many opportunities were promised to us, and big headlines on the recruitment forms said, "Opportunity to combine work and holiday!" There was a choice of three countries: Australia, Saudi Arabia and the United Kingdom.

As a child, I had grown tired of moving around. My father, who was a minister of religion, would serve as a pastor of a church for a maximum of three years, and at the end of each term, he was sent to another town. I promised myself that I would not move around when I grew up! Well, I guess travelling was now in my blood, as I was so excited about these opportunities!

As soon as I finished my degree, I was ready to apply to go to my favourite destination, which was Australia! By that time, I had gained enough experience as I had already done seven years of practical nursing in different departments, from medical, surgical and emergency to paediatrics and maternity wards.

I also got married after graduating and had a little boy. Waiting for the process was not stopping me from continuing with my life, and when the agency eventually processed my application, I had a family to consider before making any decisions about moving abroad. My husband was in the same profession, and he wanted to do specialised training, so we decided that he would do his training first. I had to change jobs and work as a community nurse to be able to have shifts that would fit my children's needs (I now had two boys). All of this meant that my application was cancelled!

Moving abroad was now dependent on whether my husband acquired the qualification he was studying for. Working in my community was such an amazing experience, and I managed to fit work in with my kids and family. I was promoted to clinic manager, and my husband finished his course and applied to go abroad! At this point, my job and my family were my pride! I was not keen on leaving my comfort zone to go somewhere that I didn't know, especially with my two children, so I told my husband how I felt about moving.

A letter arrived saying that my husband had got a job in the United Kingdom. He was excited, and he encouraged me to submit my application, but I was so busy settling down in my new position at work and being a mother. The preparations for his job started, and everything went so quickly. His company booked him an air ticket, and before we knew it, he had gone to the UK.

This was the beginning of a long journey. After only two months, my husband's employer offered me a job, so I applied for visas for myself and the boys, resigned from my job, sold our cars, took the children out of school, packed our bags and said goodbye to friends and family.

We arrived in the UK on a summer day in July. The sky was blue, but it was not warm enough for us not to wear our jumpers. Our first surprise was at the bus stop. While we were waiting for our bus on this bright, sunny day, it suddenly started raining. As is the African way, our response was to run for cover! But looking around, no one else moved! Instead, the other people waiting at the bus stop reached into their bags, pulled out their umbrellas and just carried on with their business. Back home in South Africa, we never had rain without the warning signs of dark clouds, thunder, lightning and horrible winds, all of which meant that we needed to take cover and make sure we were in a safe place.

The boys and I arrived at our new home, which was a small one-bedroom flat with an office that my husband was renting. We had the opportunity to rest for the weekend, and then early on Monday morning, I got myself ready for the interview at my husband's workplace. I was anxious because I was going to be interviewed for something slightly different since I was not registered with the nursing body and that process was going to take six months. As you can imagine, I dressed smart, hoping to make an impression and, of course, I had my work profile ready. Off I went for my interview to be a healthcare assistant.

I met the manager first thing that morning, and she allocated me to shadow a nursing assistant. Well, I did not expect to be taught how to clean bedpans and commodes, nor to be told what colour mops are to be used to mop clean areas, dirty areas and infected areas! She covered all the health and safety pros and cons and told me all about manual handling. The whole time, I was waiting for that big moment when I would be called for an interview! At 5:00pm, I was released to go home. It turned out that had been my first day of work. Well, no interview!

As I left, the manager told me to not forget my big folder that contained my profile and all my certificates. To my surprise, it had not been touched! Nobody even bothered to check what qualifications I had! "What?" I thought. "Why did I spend so many years preparing for this moment?" I grabbed my folder and walked out! My feet were killing me. I had been the only one wearing a three-quarter heel shoe; everyone else was wearing flat shoes, including the manager! My first stop was to the shoe shop to buy comfortable shoes for the next day.

At home, my kids were adjusting to their new environment, and they were happy not to be at school – it was almost the end of the school year, so there were no spaces at the schools until the beginning of the new academic year, which started in September. That meant our kids were at home for two months. This brings me to the second surprise. I was at work, and my husband was working the same shift with me when, suddenly, we were called to the manager's office and questioned about our children. We were not aware of the laws of the country, so we didn't know that leaving children alone at home was an offence. We were told that if our kids were found alone, they would be taken to social services. That was no joke! I took my bag and went home straight away. This new information put a strain on us, as we needed to have childcare if we wanted to work the same shifts.

After a month of working with my husband, I decided to look for another job that had nothing to do with caring and nursing. It was getting more and more difficult for me, and the kids also needed to have a parent around all the time. I applied for a job as a sewing machinist in another city. It was a nine to five job, which meant I could drop the kids off at school in the morning and pick them up after work. My husband looked for a house near my new workplace and not far from a school for the children. We moved into our new home and managed to settle down in a decent habitat, in a good neighbourhood, and with a proper bedroom for the boys.

Everybody was happy besides my husband who was not enjoying work at all. The things that were happening every day were making him very uneasy. I can remember one day, when I dropped him off at work, he stood outside looking at me and the kids as though he wanted to go back home. After four months working there, it came as no surprise that his boss asked him not to come back to work … not because he had done anything wrong but because his boss wanted to protect him from his colleagues who were ganging up against him because he was African. That was the most devastating time of our stay in England. My husband was at home for two months without a job, but he was paid – as promised – until he got another job.

After he got a new job, I received my nursing registration number and was then able to apply for a job as a nurse. This came with a few challenges, as we needed childcare again. We made friends at church, and some of those friends were able to help. We enrolled our children at a Christian school, and they were happy in that friendly environment. My husband also started studying at a Bible College, and things seemed to be going as planned. Meanwhile, we were now looking at our personal lives, because after three years in the UK, I fell pregnant and gave birth to a baby girl! We had to move to a bigger house to accommodate the new addition to the family. Life was taking its turn, but not in the way we had planned when we applied to work abroad.

Eventually, I joined a private company that was providing community services; I worked as a community nurse, and this was my most desired job. The experience of travelling and seeing the English culture was great, and it made me realise and embrace the true sense of who I am as a person. I came to appreciate that I am who I am, and it cannot be changed.

I had the privilege of visiting my patients in their homes. This taught me the English culture from its origins, in places where nothing could be changed or hidden. I learned to respect the English for who they are, and I came to understand that some conditions become acceptable to them because of their backgrounds and their living spaces. In particular, having elderly live-in parents is very difficult due to limited space. And so, instead of cursing them for sending their parents to old age homes, I understood that the system pushes them in that direction.

Raising kids in a foreign country was a challenge. I wanted to bring them up in the way I was brought up in Africa, but the culture around me did not agree with what I thought was right. Back home it was easier because we had the support of our family. And hiring a nanny is much cheaper in Africa than in the UK.

There is one thing I could not understand about the English system: that there is no respect for someone's hard work. A person can lose everything without any proper evidence of the events. Many lose their practice licence, driving licence, marriage licence, parenthood and some even lose their kids to social services. When I started working as a sewing machinist, I worked with an English qualified nurse. I could hardly believe what she told me – she had stopped practising as a nurse because of some issues at work. It seems that the English have no consideration of someone's achievements in life – they are ignored or destroyed at the drop of a hat. Saying that, I do agree with the fact that we need to respect the laws of the country. However, in most cases, people are treated as machines and not as humans and, therefore, errors are unacceptable, and that limits the room for someone to learn and improve.

I say this from experience as I have seen people in my country who had 'issues' at work and were demoted. We used to see them scrubbing the floors until they were re-trained and they had learned their lesson. But they did not lose everything, and they didn't lose all the knowledge they acquired while training and re-training. What changed was their behaviour and attitude, and so, their families still survived.

I am grateful for the opportunity that I had in coming to the UK. If I were to start life again, I think I would still migrate, only I'd do certain things differently!

16

My Life in Diaspora Story

I came to the United Kingdom after completing a psychology degree in Zimbabwe but not being able to find a job. I arrived on Christmas Day on a six-week visitor's visa visiting my aunt and her family. When I had three weeks left on my visa, family and friends advised me to consult an immigration lawyer about extending it, and a lawyer assisted me with an application to extend my visa to six months. While waiting for the extension, I started applying for a yearlong access course to nursing. During that time, I moved in with my sister and her family and found a part-time job to fund the college fees. It was such an overwhelming experience as I was working illegally; my visitor's visa did not permit me to work, and I was working for more than forty-eight hours per week to raise the finances needed. It was a gamble between being caught and deported by immigration officials and raising money to enrol in college and study for a new career. After three months, fortunately, my visitor's visa was extended, and at the same time, I was accepted on the access course.

At the start of my studies, I applied for a twelve-month student visa, and it was granted within two months. Soon after, I had to move out of my sister's home and find my own accommodation, pay my own bills and raise further fees so that I could study nursing at university. It was such a challenge. Attending college and working full-time was hard work, but I persevered. I applied for a degree in psychiatric nursing and was invited to attend two interviews. I chose this type of nursing because I have an innate passion for helping people with mental health problems. The first interview was at a local university. I attended the interview but, unfortunately, was not successful. I was really frustrated and deeply troubled because I had my heart set on studying there. I was offered a place at the other university on the condition that I pay my fees as an international student, but this university was two hundred miles away, and I didn't want to be that far away from my family.

I am a Christian, so I've always had faith in God, but during this time, my faith was tried and tested remarkably. I found myself becoming very anxious, emotional, sad and upset, just to mention a few negative emotions. I realised that the only way that I would overcome was to put all of my confidence, hope, trust, and unshakeable, unwavering and stubborn faith in God.

I remember very well how I broke down in my access class one day. I cried sincere and heartfelt tears because I was among the few who had not been offered a position to study nursing at the local university. My tutor was moved with my desire and passion, and what she did next really touched my heart. She contacted the university directly and kindly asked them to consider inviting me for another interview. And they agreed! It was such a dream come true, and a real miracle. When I went for the interview, I said my prayers and trusted God to make a way, as always. Thank God, I received an offer to study at that university, and as an added bonus, I was informed that the government would pay my tuition fees! I was grateful because I knew that upon completing my degree, I would get a decent and good job.

When I commenced my nursing degree, I applied for a three-year visa, and it was granted within two months. Once again, I faced the challenge of being a full-time student and a full-time employee. I had two jobs: one as a support worker, looking after people with learning disabilities in their own homes, and the other as a healthcare assistant with an agency. It was hard work, but I needed two jobs to cover all of my expenses and support my parents and five siblings in Zimbabwe (my father had lost his job due to the tough economic conditions). Sometimes, I would spend all day at college, and then work a night shift, only to return to college the next morning for another full day's study. In hindsight, I believe this was possible through God's unmerited favour and grace. It kept me going, and I never considered giving up.

All the hard work paid off, and I proudly completed my studies with a first-class honours bachelor's degree. However, I could not get a job as a qualified nurse, not even in a nursing home, because at that time, the British Home Office was not processing work permits for non-European citizens. It left me with mixed feelings; I was happy and joyous that I had successfully finished my degree, but I was anxious and self-piteous about the job situation. I was offered many posts by hospitals and nursing homes, but all offers were later withdrawn as my work permits were not approved. It was extremely frustrating. When I had only four months of legal stay left on my student visa, I started applying to other countries as a registered nurse since I had no hope of getting a job in Britain. I applied to the Republic of Ireland, Australia and Canada. The other obvious alternative was to go back to Zimbabwe, but I could not imagine doing this, even as a last resort, because the unemployment level was at its highest and the economy was in a crisis with very high inflation rates.

As if that was not enough trouble and misery, my fiancé of three years also walked out on me as we could not reach an agreement over a jointly owned property in Zimbabwe. T he relationship had been rocky as he emotionally and psychologically abused me throughout the three years – he was very controlling, insensitive, insecure, jealous and manipulative. The day before he left, I had asked church elders to come to our house to mediate in a bid to reconcile our differences. The following morning, he turned up with his uncle, his brother and a van. With tears streaming down my cheeks, I begged him to stay and told him that the elders were coming to pray and counsel us, but heartlessly, he told me that the relationship was over and there was no changing his mind. It was like a double blow. On the one hand, I could not find a job, and on the other hand, my fiancé left me when I needed him the most. I cried day and night, and I felt like the world had turned upside down. I could not see even a glimmer of light at the end of the tunnel.

Two months before my student visa was due to expire, I was offered a job at one of the leading hospitals in Ireland. It was a great relief! Yet, it was still frustrating because I had to wait for all the relevant paperwork to be processed. This included registering with the Irish Nurses and Midwives Organisation as well as undertaking health screenings, such as routine blood tests and chest x-rays. While waiting for my paperwork, I continued working as a healthcare assistant, which was a bitter pill to swallow to a large extent, as I was working alongside my former college mates even though I was now qualified. However, I just had to accept it because I had no other option. One month before my visa expired, my finances were challenged. Before my fiancé had left, he changed all the utility bills into my name, making me liable to pay them. Now, I was struggling – I could not afford my rent. But thanks be to God, my sister saw my need and didn't turn a blind eye, and she invited me to stay with her again.

This was a very challenging time as I experienced a lot of negative emotions. I felt let down by the British system and, strictly speaking, I used to ask, "Why did they bother training me as a nurse only to send me away with my acquired skills and expertise to practice as a qualified nurse elsewhere?" To cope with these negative feelings of sadness, self-pity and shame, once again, I turned to God. I realised that no one other than God Himself knew the way out of the challenges I was facing. I reminded myself that my breakthrough would only come if I persisted in fighting the 'good fight of faith' as written about in the Bible. As someone who was raised with a strong Christian influence, I knew that I could trust God, and I was convinced that He had neither abandoned me nor would He put me to shame. This belief really kept me going. I also received a lot of support from fellow church members who encouraged me through prayer and study of the Bible.

There were significant delays in the processing of my paperwork to relocate to Ireland so, unfortunately, my student visa expired. I ended up being an illegal immigrant in the UK. It was a daunting experience living with this knowledge. If caught, I would be deported, and I would go back to Zimbabwe with nothing, as all my savings would be frozen. I could do nothing else but continue to trust God for the outcome and believe that He would turn things around for my good.

When the paperwork was finally ready, I encountered another very stressful challenge! According to the European immigration laws, if a non-European wants to relocate to another European country, that person must have a valid visa from the departing country with at least three months' remaining. The problem was that my UK student visa had expired four months earlier, so when I went to the Irish embassy, I was refused an Irish travel visa. In fact, I was told to go back to Zimbabwe and re-apply. But I could not even contemplate doing this because I had no guarantee that Zimbabwean officials would grant me a work visa to return to Ireland.

As desperate situations call for desperate measures, I recall attempting to send my documents and passport to my parents in Zimbabwe via DHL. I placed a fifty-euro note for the visa application inside my passport. However, the DHL agent discovered it, and he sternly told me that sending money with documents is not permitted, as per their policy. Tears streamed down my cheeks, and I went back to my sister's house feeling hopeless and helpless.

I quickly realised that I had tried to work things out for myself, and had forgotten to trust God in this situation. I repented and dug my heels in deeper, determined to trust God and depend upon Him, and not my own efforts. I went back to the Irish embassy for the second time, and truly, my ever faithful God and Father made a way – my application for a visa was approved!

Just five days later, I arrived in Ireland. I was on a work permit for five years and had no problems in renewing my visa on a yearly basis. According to the Irish immigration laws, if someone has been on a work permit for five years and has resided in the state continuously, they qualify for citizenship. The last time that I renewed my visa before I could make this application for citizenship, I did so two days late because I could not get an appointment in time. As I was about to leave the immigration centre, I mentioned to the officer that I was going to apply for citizenship the following year. He informed me that I would not qualify because I had been two days late and, therefore, had not complied with the renewal terms. However, he gently asked me to give him my passport, and he changed the renewal date on my visa so that there were no gaps in the work permit! A year later, I applied for my citizenship, and there were no issues or concerns expressed. I was granted Irish citizenship. I give thanks to God for I believe He showed me His favour and goodness in that situation, and it reminded me of the scripture that says, 'If God is for us, who can be against us?'

In conclusion, these testimonies and breakthroughs have strengthened my faith. I can testify that I have seen, felt, tasted, heard and smelled God's endless compassion, goodness, new mercies, unmerited favour, kindness, faithfulness, power, and unabated and unconditional love in my life. Indeed, God has been ever faithful and has always been shining the light of His face upon me. Hence, I can boldly declare that He is my Ebenezer, the Lord who has brought me this far and who will continue to walk by my side all the days of my blessed and precious life. I have come to the full knowledge that nothing happens in a Christians' life by accident, chance or coincidence; hence, the Bible encourages us to be strong and courageous, for all things will always work out for our good, according to God's special timing and purpose in our lives.

I trust that my story will touch, encourage and inspire many people with immigration or other challenging circumstances. There is never a hopeless situation because God can turn around any situation for His glory and names' sake. We simply need to turn to Him and cast all our cares on Him, for He truly cares for us, and He has an excellent plan and purpose for all of our lives. I have learned never to give up in life, but to believe in myself, persevere, work hard, and leave the rest to God for He is the extraordinary strategist. He has declared our end from the beginning and knows tomorrow from today. Therefore, I will always proclaim that all is and shall always be well with me and my household in Jesus' mighty name.

Conclusion

L eaving livelihoods, partners, family, friends and children so that one's future can be enhanced by living in diaspora is a never an easy decision to make. Not only do migrants have to adjust to differences in weather, culture and language, sort out employment and accommodation, and deal with changes to family dynamics and challenges with childcare, but they also take their responsibilities to their relatives back home very seriously.

In pursuit of a better future for themselves and their families, many are driven to risk all they have and travel without valid visas and adequate paperwork. Some enter a country under false presences, fearing they will be deported at the airport. Most search for work from day one, even without work permits, because the alternative of sitting back and waiting for the permits is unbearable to contemplate – much time would be wasted. Many seize the opportunities of employers who are willing to employ them while waiting for their immigration papers to be approved. Not knowing if the visa will be granted or if one will be discovered working illegally is another risk that countless are willing to take. While a lot of migrants are deported for working without relevant permits, there are equally just as many who have been fortunate to escape being detained and deported simply by not attending certain meetings or interviews.

* * *

The contributors to this book have had similar experiences. None of them travelled to a foreign land to scrounge or misuse the benefits system; most made the journey to work and study, and all were willing to do whatever it took to fend for themselves and their families left behind.

Many lived in diaspora for a long time without permission to reside or work, all the while fighting immigration battles with lawyers and immigration officers. Yet, despite this black cloud looming over their shoulders each day, they got up, went to work and did all they could to continue to work and send money home to support their families. Usually, this meant working in menial jobs, even though they had already gained skills and work experience from senior posts in their home countries. In 2014, people living in diaspora sent over $32 billion to the sub-Saharan Africa, which is a staggering amount benefitting the countries from which most immigrants originate.[1]

In addition to the menial jobs, several of our contributors sacrificed their privileged lifestyles, one where they could afford

---

1 https://qz.com/389111/diaspora-sent-32-9-billion-home-to-sub-saharan-africa-in-2014 [accessed September 2018]

a cleaner, a nanny and a driver, only to live in cramped shared accommodation.

Ultimately, some had to wait more than 8 years for their visa.

While some of our contributors entered a new country with the purpose of studying, others decided it was the only way to gain a visa. Regardless, those who pursued their studies are now in full-time employment and are contributing to the economy of the country in which they now reside. For most, visas and work permits have not been a problem and the majority of them are now citizens of those countries. Due to bursaries being offered to study nursing, many flocked to study this profession, and for this funding, many are extremely appreciative. Some succeeded and gained qualifications only to be stranded at the end; since their student visas had expired, no one wanted to employ them without the right permits. They ended up applying for work elsewhere and had to migrate to other countries. To those it affected, it seemed such a loss to the country that funded them to study a 3-year degree, only for their skills to benefit another nation and economy. All that people who have migrated to diaspora want is to be able to work legally, study, gain qualifications, and support themselves and their families back home.[2] They also want to be able to freely travel back and forth to their home country without the fear of deportation; they don't want to wait 8 years or more to be granted a work permit or indefinite leave to remain status. While immigrants appreciate that there are many factors

---

2 https://fullfact.org/immigration/why-do-international-migrants-come-uk [accessed September 2018]

at play, we hope that one day, the processing of visas and permits will move much quicker so that those who genuinely want to work are not hindered in their efforts. After all, paying taxes to the receiving country can only benefit the economy.

Several of our contributors were initially funded by friends and families, but that didn't guarantee their well-being. One lady had her passport locked away, and another lived without heating in the middle of winter. It's unfortunate! As people in diaspora, we ought to treat each other with dignity, as we would like to be treated. What is there gain from someone else's misery and sorrow when we are all in the same boat in diaspora? Let us lead by example and *"be the change we want to see in the world."* (Mahatma Gandhi).

Unfortunately, some have been taken advantage of by those left behind in their country of origin. Relentless messages asked for help with school fees, repairs, business ventures, rent, clothes, food, medical aid and funerals. In some cases, the money was not used for these stated purposes but to fund their pampering! Have the people in diaspora created co-dependent relationships with people back home? Maybe. While our relatives and friends are in desperate situations and need help, have they become dependent on us, and therefore incapable of being self-sufficient?

Many in diaspora have realised that money does not grow on trees, they only wish those back home would understand it. Immigrants work very hard, sometimes day and night to earn every penny to sustain themselves in diaspora and send back home. If family members are genuinely struggling or elderly parents need taking care of, or if there is an emergency, that's different. There is still high unemployment, high inflation and political uncertainty in some developing countries, but we must ask how others survive in such conditions without financial support from overseas. These people are able to find work and provide for themselves, so should we not be encouraging our friends and family to be self-sufficient and consider sustainability long-term? What will happen when those in diaspora are no longer able to keep sending money back home? Will their relatives perish? Or will they adapt and do what it takes to have all the necessities they need? Surely, given enough time, all mankind can adapt to anything, just as people in diaspora have adapted to living in new countries, with different cultures, jobs and languages. Many have already adapted and are thriving in the countries from which they migrated.[3] As they say, *"Give a man a fish, and you feed him for a day; teach a man to fish, and you feed him for a lifetime."* (Chinese proverb). Probably, it's time we start working collaboratively with those back home and start teaching them to fish for themselves, rather than keep giving them fish.

Several contributors have questioned whether they should stay in diaspora or return home. The yearning to return home rarely diminishes; there is a yearning to re-invest in the country of their birth, and there is an unending hope that situations improve enough so that they can return to their families and help rebuild their countries by sharing and applying the skills and knowledge they have gained in diaspora. But as time passes by, one cannot

---

3 https://www.kidsnewtocanada.ca/culture/adaptation
[accessed September 2018]

help but be distanced from their country of origin; so much has changed, family members have dispersed around the world, and some have passed away. What remains to return to?

Conversely, most are happy with their new lives in diaspora and have accepted that home is where they are! They have bought houses, married, divorced, met new partners, started families and brought their families to come and live with them. Some have studied new courses, degrees, master's programmes and PhDs. Yet, despite being well educated, many face challenges of discrimination, resulting in limited career progression opportunities. Immigrants desire to be accepted in society, to be treated equally, to be valued and respected, having access to employment and career prospects; they do not want to be stigmatised or discriminated against because of their names, accent, the colour of their skin or ethnicity.

* * *

Certainly, living in diaspora has its highs and lows, as you have heard from these candid stories. For our contributors to have thrived in diaspora, they had to adapt and work with sheer determination and perseverance. They never gave up, even when doors were slammed in their faces, and even with the fear of getting caught without immigration permits. Undoubtedly, this courageousness led them to achieve their dreams and goals, and they continue supporting their families back home.

We can never ignore the media's outcry that immigrants are taking jobs away from the citizens of the country.[4] But, surely, if these jobs were filled, immigrants would not have been able to find these jobs? Many industries are dependent on immigrants; so much so, that without them, these industries would struggle to sustain their systems.

Let us, as people of a worldwide community, embrace each other, not discriminate against each other. *"…beneath the skin, beyond the differing features and into the true heart of being, fundamentally we are all more alike, my friend, than we are unalike."* (Maya Angelou). *"We all need to treat each other with human dignity and respect."* (Madonna).

* * *

Thank you for taking the time to travel the world by reading these stories of living in diaspora. If you are an immigrant, we hope you have been inspired, challenged and encouraged that you are not alone. Many have gone before you, and many will follow. There are others who can help you just as much as you can help another. If you are not an immigrant, we hope that you have learned something new about living in diaspora and that you have gained some understanding of what challenges migrants have faced and will continue to endure. And maybe

---

4 https://www.theguardian.com/politics/2016/nov/03/people-moving-to-uk-arent-taking-british-jobs-says-george-osborne [accessed September 2018]; https://www.bbc.co.uk/news/business-37577620 [accessed September 2018]

your own views and opinions of people living in diaspora have been challenged, and even changed.

Change will not come if we wait
for some other person or some other time.
We are the ones we've been waiting for.
We are the change that we seek.

BARACK OBAMA

Share with Us!

———————

We hope you have been challenged and inspired by the stories in this book. Whether or not you can identify with our contributors, we hope you have been able to empathise with immigrants living in diaspora and that you have enjoyed reading this book as much as we have enjoyed compiling and writing it. We would love to hear your thoughts, reactions or comments to any of the stories. Please get in touch: **admin@talesindiaspora.com**

* * *

For more information about this book, to join our mailing list or to follow us on social media, please visit: **www.talesindiaspora.com**

About the Authors

———

Audry Msipa and Grace Maworera are both healthcare professionals who have lived in diaspora for the past 18 years. Their own experiences and challenges of immigration sparked their passion for sharing the stories of others in the same position. Fundamentally, the message they desire to communicate is that people living in diaspora are not alone and that they can overcome challenges with hard work and perseverance, causing them to succeed in their different journeys and reach their desired goals.

Audry and Grace are also co-owners of a publishing company and a private investment company. They currently live with their families in the UK and Ireland, respectively.